T0210124

"This has to be one of the most practical devotionals I have read in fifty years of ministry. It is rich in content, deep in truth, steeped in Scripture and distilled through experience. The vulnerability and honesty of the writer gives the reader the permission to be real. I have always believed that 95% of the will of God is sanctified common sense, and this book, viewed through the lens of godly and practical wisdom, becomes essential reading for anyone who is serious about aligning their daily walk with God with His best intentions for them. I cannot recommend this wonderful work too highly"

John Glass
General Superintendent Elim Pentecostal Churches, UK
(2000-2016)
Chair of Council, Evangelical Alliance, UK (2014-2018)

Dr. Carol Alexander is an extremely gifted communicator, educator, and author. Her love for life and the Giver of Life are contagious. You will be intrigued and inspired by the interesting array of topics she covers in her devotional. Each chapter is relevant and practical as she illustrates the truth of God's Word with personal illustrations from a lifelong journey of faith. Your spirit will be renewed as you examine the Scriptures through the lens of this insightful author.

Mark Dean
Superintendent, Minnesota District, Assemblies of God

Carol Alexander reflects on passages and principles of Scripture with an engaging blend of interpretive skill and personal transparency. The format is refreshingly non-linear. Readers are not discouraged from taking a start-to-finish approach, but invited to explore the texts and topics of particular chapters in whatever order aligns with their life experiences or current circumstances. *Simple Trust: Fifty Life Changing Readings* delivers on its title. We commend it to all, like us, who hold on to hope as we walk the road of pain and promise.

Dr. Mike and Faith Beals
President, Vanguard University

Dr. Carol's devotional is an honest, vulnerable, adventurous and inspirational journey of trusting God at every twist & turn, on every mountain top and in every valley. Carol masterfully unpacks the wisdom and grace that flows out of trusting God to make sense of the pace and complexity of living a full life! One thing I know and love about Carol is her unwavering integrity! She is a woman who, in her walk with Jesus, in her leadership and her speaking relentlessly pursues God's truth, knowing it is only in who He is, that true trust can find a home!

DJ McPhail
Lead Pastor Liberty church, Randburg, South Africa

Simple Trust

FIFTY LIFE CHANGING READINGS

Carol Anne Alexander

WESTBOW
PRESS*
A DIVISION OF THOMAS NELSON
& ZONDERVAN

WestBow Press books may be ordered through booksellers or by contacting:

WestBow Press
A Division of Thomas Nelson & Zondervan
1663 Liberty Drive
Bloomington, IN 47403
www.westbowpress.com
1 (866) 928-1240

Interior Image Credit: Rich Schwarz

Scriptures taken from the Holy Bible, New International Version®, NIV®.
Copyright © 1973, 1978, 1984, 2011 by Biblica, Inc.™ Used by permission
of Zondervan. All rights reserved worldwide. www.zondervan.com
The "NIV" and "New International Version" are trademarks registered
in the United States Patent and Trademark Office by Biblica, Inc.™

ISBN: 978-1-9736-9256-0 (sc)
ISBN: 978-1-9736-9258-4 (hc)
ISBN: 978-1-9736-9257-7 (e)

Library of Congress Control Number: 2020909510

Print information available on the last page.

WestBow Press rev. date: 5/28/2020

For
Ava and Tylan:
Two of the most precious gifts God gave me.
I love you to the moon and back.
Let *Simple Trust* in Jesus guide and lead you to your destinies.

Contents

Foreword

As a wife, mom, mimi, leader, and minister, the frenetic pace of trying to get it all done can feel overwhelming. I've learned that no other place fills the well of my soul except time in His Word and in His presence. In today's culture, the noise of busyness and constant hurry seem to continually shout at us. The distracting clamor threatens to drown out the Holy Spirit's whisper, beckoning us to draw away and meet with God. The Lord created your spirit and mine with a built-in hunger and thirst for Him. Our soul longs for the peace His presence brings. In Christ alone, we discover our ultimate purpose and find the truth that transforms us every day.

We need simple tools to direct our gaze to Jesus. Throughout many seasons of my life, I have relied on devotionals, written by people I admire and trust, to help me apply God's Word each day. This beautiful collection of reflective devotionals, penned by Dr. Carol Alexander, prompts us to navigate well this one life we've been given here on earth. Carol's quick mind, articulate voice, and biblical perspective—seasoned through a lifetime of passionately following Jesus—will pull you into every scenario she shares. *Simple Trust* is a timely resource that invites us to come away from this busy, chaotic world, into the secret place with the Lord. If you read this devotional with a desire to grasp truth, reflect, and apply it to your life, *Simple Trust* just might become your favorite companion for your daily time with God.

Kay Burnett, Women's Ministry Director, Assemblies of God, USA

Preface

They that trust in the Lord shall never be confounded!
—George Muller

For the past fifty years, I have walked a journey with God that has impacted every part of my life. Each layer of this adventure has been filled with varying shades of color.

There have been dark days when the weight of my heart felt too heavy for my chest. These were the worst of times for me. Someone once said, that adversity introduces you to yourself. Nothing has helped me to know the real me as much as my pain. At times, negative thoughts bumped about in my head, and I felt that my trust would be swept away by them, but when the clatter stilled, the Lord was there. Doubts too have permeated the fabric of my life, but simple trust would fill my heart and wash them away, even when they whispered in the corridors of my mind.

There have been many happy days where simple trust has invaded my soul so that I felt as if nothing was impossible. God's love would envelop my heart and melt away past anguish like sunshine on snowflakes. I love those days.

The mundane and routine days are the ones I like least. Those are the times where I simply have to persevere, but all of these days have textured my life, making me the person I am today. And it is out of all these colorful experiences that I write this devotional.

Some of the Bible readings in this devotional contain an entire chapter or portions of chapters. At times, you may wonder what they have to do with the devotional, but I want the readings to give you a context to what I am writing about, even if the entire chapter does not fit precisely with my writing.

I have written with honesty and vulnerability, and my hope is that the same simple trust that has grown in my heart over six decades will take root in yours. Blaise Pascal said, "Once your soul has been enlarged by a truth, it can never return to its original size." It is true that when you open your heart to truth, it has a profound and lasting impact on you.

Truth comes wrapped in a variety of ways. At times, it is clothed in pain and sorrow, and on other occasions in joy and strength. Even in the midst of grief, beauty can spring forth like wildflowers in the desert. Sometimes, trust grows more in the soil of grief and produces a beauty that could never have otherwise occurred. Henry Ward Beecher said, "We are always on the anvil; by trials God is shaping us for higher things." God can take an unformed and unsightly lump of clay and turn it into something of rare beauty. The only condition is that the clay is yielded to the Potter. As you confront truth in each devotional, may your soul be enlarged and transformed.

This is a devotional with a difference. You can open this book to any page and start reading. Be unconventional if you want. You do not have to go from the first to the final page, although if you do, that is perfectly fine. Each devotional speaks to some personal experience in my life and journey with the Lord. I have been encouraged to take these pithy narratives that are intrinsically part of my journey and share them with a wider audience.

My devotional handles a diverse and eclectic number of subjects. These reflect on raw, earthy, and complex issues that we all face over time. As you process what I have written, I hope you will have the courage to respond in a way that will enrich your life and the lives of those around you.

Each devotion concludes with a reflection, and I hope that these will be helpful. *Reflection* may sound abstract, or to some, it may even appear mystical. We often reflect when our minds are not engaged in some activity and are free to roam wherever they choose. The reflections in this book are more deliberate and intentional, with the purpose of being still and quiet. I love what Blaise Pascal said about this: "Most of man's troubles come from his inability to be still." These reflections are designed for you to pause, to give careful consideration to what you have read, and then react appropriately. I trust that as you respond to each devotion, you will experience the transformation of life that comes from submitting to the God Who loves you. The short prayer at the conclusion of each devotion is simply to guide you in your own expression to God.

I hope that these musings will fill you with simple trust as you journey with the Lord. Wherever you are in your own walk, my hope is that that you will make room for God so that trust will fill every crevice of your soul, and your love for God will be deeply enhanced.

I have come to understand that trust is not an intangible or mysteriously unreachable goal. It is simple and yet profound.

I am, and always will be, recklessly abandoned, ruthlessly committed, and in relentless pursuit of Jesus.

Carol

Seize the Day

 Reading: Philippians 4

As I grow older, time seems to grow wings and fly as fast as a cheetah chasing its prey. Time is one of the most precious resources we have, and it is often the most abused. Sometimes, I wish I could capture time, lock it up, and lose the key. I know I cannot, but I can seize each moment and make the best of every day.

I love this season of my life so much that it seems each hour is being swallowed up. I look at my grandchildren and wish I could freeze the moments I have with them. They were my sweet little babies only a few years ago, and now they are growing children.

Yesterday is gone. The past can never be recaptured, and we are not assured of tomorrow, but we can engage today to the best of our ability. The apostle Paul exhorted the church in Philippi, "Rejoice in the Lord always. I will say it again: Rejoice" (Philippians 4:4). Rejoicing, according to the aged apostle, was a choice. Further on, the apostle claims in Philippians 4:11, "I have learned to be content whatever the circumstances." He augments this teaching further by saying that he knew what it was to be in need or to have plenty. Whether he was well fed or hungry, he had learned the discipline of being content in every situation. What a secure and comfortable place to be.

Perhaps the circumstances surrounding you right now are less than favorable. However, despite what you are facing at this moment, be encouraged by these verses and choose to live a life of joy.

Life is fleeting, and we can never be sure of tomorrow. James 4:14 says, "Why, you don't even know what will happen tomorrow. What is your life? You are a mist that appears for a little while and then vanishes." The brevity of life is a sobering thought. It inspires me to capture each moment, to inhale deeply, and exhale slowly. I want to lick the dish clean and end my life well. Simply put: I want to seize this day.

There are three ways I don't want to end my days.

First, I don't want to end my life with regrets. Reflecting back, I don't want to feel sorrow for wasted moments. My desire is to live each day to the fullest. In the evening, when I lie on my bed and close my eyes, I want to smile about the day I have lived and sleep deeply because I have lived fully.

Second, I don't want to end my life with unfinished tasks. Like everyone else, I have dreams, and I want to accomplish them. Some dreams are unrealistic, but the ones worth pursuing are the ones I want to achieve before I stand before Jesus and give Him an account of my life. It doesn't matter how old I am; I still have dreams and desires in my heart for tomorrow. I never want to stop dreaming.

Third, I don't want to end my life with unforgiveness in my heart or holding grudges against people. My desire is to live life void of bitterness and anger, and to do this, I must keep short accounts with everyone. Each moment I am alive, I want a free heart and a joyful spirit.

How do we seize this day and live with a joyful heart, as apostle Paul encouraged us to? Here are four principles that can help you achieve this goal:

- Living with an attitude of joy takes discipline. When you wake up in the morning, is your heart filled with gratitude and joy for what you have, or are you thinking about all the things you want and don't have? Think about it for a moment. You are alive, breathing God's air, and you have all the possibilities this day holds for you; that should fill you with thankfulness. We assume that happiness or joy is dependent upon our circumstances. Of course, our circumstances can greatly enhance our joy. However, this simple and yet profound text found in Philippians 4:4 states plainly that we should always rejoice. In other words, despite the circumstances surrounding us, we can and should choose to be joyful. We choose joy because we are alive, we have the potential of the day, and we have a God Who loves us and holds our future in His hands.

- Comparison and competition diminish joy and gratitude. When we measure our lives against someone else's, we are in danger of diminishing who we are. Comparing ourselves with others or competing with them is not good for our own self-worth. We sometimes wonder why we don't have what other people have. We think we are deserving of more. Real and lasting joy comes from being content in your own skin and being thankful for the life you have. Remember that someone else's life can look perfect to you, but you have never had to walk in their shoes; you don't know the struggle and heartache they are dealing with. It never helps to compare yourself with others. You should be grateful for what you have and for the life you are living.

- Peace follows on the heels of gratitude. Until we become satisfied with our lot in life, we will never experience the peace that Jesus promised: "Peace I leave with you; my peace I give you. I do not give to you as the world gives. Do not let your hearts be troubled and do not be afraid" (John 14:27). The peace that Jesus gives is not the same peace that people experience in the world; it is a peace unlike any we have known before. Some may feel a sense of peace when their bank account is flourishing, when they have material wealth, or when they achieved some accomplishment or received an accolade. The peace Jesus talks about is one that comes from finding satisfaction in Him, not in things, experiences, or accomplishments. It is a peace that we can experience even in the midst of difficult or trying circumstances. Look around you, and be thankful for what you have: family and friends, a clear mind, food to eat and clothes to wear, and a God Who is always there for you.

I have travelled the world and realize how blessed many of us in the West are. I have seen little children in Africa with skeletal bodies and paper-thin skin. These little ones are not assured of even one meal in the week. Most of us reading this devotional anticipate filling our bellies with the food of our choice during the course of each day. Some people live in war-torn nations or are being persecuted because they are Christians. In the West, we have the freedom to read our Bibles and go to church without the thought of persecution.

Christ followers around the globe often experience some type of injustice. Justice is not always easy to achieve in this world. Lies often cover the truth, oppression can crush freedom, and violence can and often does silence the voice of protest. There are times when life is unfair. When I bemoan the circumstances of my life, I take stock, pause, and think about people who live in extreme circumstances with far less than I have, and it puts my life in perspective. Despite the challenges of life, we can still know the peace that Jesus offers, even in the midst of an unjust world. This peace can sustain us in trial and pain.

- Joy and gratitude go hand in hand. I have never met a joy-filled person who is not a grateful person. There are no two words I love to hear more than *thank you*. I have an inkling that God enjoys hearing those words from our lips. It seems to me that many people living in the comfortable West take much for granted. We live in an age of entitlement and are apt to say, "I want," but "Thank you" does not come as easily. Pause for a few moments, and count your blessings. You may be surprised at how numerous they are.

You do not have a choice as to how each day will unfold; however, you can choose your responses and attitude in each situation. Allow gratitude to seep into your soul and refresh it with hope. Choose to live this day to the fullest with a free and happy heart. Accomplish the task at hand, and strive to do better and more. Never allow time to be your master or become its slave. Choose well.

Reflection

Write down three things you are grateful for. Now list a few of the most important people in your life, and reflect on how they have contributed to your well-being. Thank God for each one of these people. Think of a new opportunity you can take today and strive to achieve it. How will you seize this day?

Prayer

God, thank You for a new day and the opportunities it presents. Thank You for the simple things of life—food, clean water, clothing, and family. As I face the challenges before me, I pray for Your guidance and Your help. Above all else, I pray that my heart will be filled with joy and gratitude throughout this day and that I will seize each moment. Drench my heart with simple trust and help me to live in a way that honors You.

Keep on Keeping On

 Reading: Philippians 3:13–17

How many times do we set new goals at the beginning of a year, and before the first week is over, we have forgotten them or failed?

The other day, a coworker came to my office and asked, while casually leaning against my door, "What are your future goals?" I did not need to go rushing through the corridors of my mind searching for an answer. We had recently been given a ten-week sabbatical, and it had given me time for reflection. So in one sense, I had been doing some soul searching, but I was able to say without hesitation, "To keep on doing what I am doing with a happy heart." I decided a long time ago what my goal in life was, and I want to stay committed to that goal with a joy-filled heart.

One of the challenges in life is to keep going, day after day. In other words, staying consistent in the midst of the mundane and routine can be difficult, but it can also be rewarding. There are probably times in life when you want to throw in the towel. I know there's been more than one occasion when I wanted to pack up and go to some distant land where no one would find me. But one of the wisest decisions we can make is to get up each morning and keep on keeping on. The question is, how do we keep on going when the going gets tough? Here are a few suggestions:

Keep your eye on the goal. Don't get distracted by the things around you. Athletes know the importance of keeping their eye on the finishing line. Some have lost critical races in a moment of distraction. The same is true in our Christian race. Your circumstances may not be optimal, but your purpose is to press on toward the goal, to win the prize from our Bible reading today. One of the best ways to accomplish this is to leave the past behind. Don't keep dredging up your failures (or your successes). Today is a new day, and you need to focus on the goal in front of you; don't keep looking in the rearview mirror.

- Remember where your help comes from. The psalmist put it beautifully when he said in Psalm 121:2, "My help comes from the Lord, the Maker of heaven and earth." We sometimes look for help in all the wrong places. People will fail us, our circumstances can suddenly change, the economy can take a dive and leave us in a predicament, but we can put our trust in the Lord, Who never changes. This is the simple trust I exhort you to explore in your devotion and walk with the Lord.

- Don't allow discouragement to steal your future. How many times have people given up because they failed? Sometimes, our failures are what make us better. Consider for a moment the great scientist Albert Einstein. He gave us the theory of relativity and deepened our understanding of how the universe works. He also won the Nobel Prize in 1921, as well as creating the beginnings of quantum theory. Did you know that prior to all his achievements, he was considered a failure? He did not speak until the age of four, and he failed his entrance exam into the Swiss Federal Polytechnic School. He did eventually graduate from university, but he struggled and nearly dropped out on numerous occasions because of his poor performance. Probably the hardest of all the burdens to bear was that his father considered him a failure. To his credit, he didn't give up but kept on keeping on. And today, we have his legacy. What legacy will you leave behind? Getting up each morning and being faithful to the task at hand is what got Einstein to his goal. Don't allow discouragement to rob you of your tomorrow. Keep on keeping on.

- If you fall down, get up and try again. Someone once said that if you fall ten times, get up ten times; just ensure that you keep falling towards your goal. Failure doesn't spell the end; it often gets us closer to our goal. Don't let your failure define your future; rather, let it propel you toward a better one. I know people who have given up on their goal because they failed the first time. Other people I know have kept on trying, even when they failed over and over, but because they never gave up, they ultimately reached their goal. Which person will you be?
- Keep a happy heart. Yes, even in the midst of failure, you can get up with a smile. The point is that you don't lose heart but keep a joyful disposition. As I already noted in our previous devotion, being happy and content is a choice that we can make.

So if life feels mundane and stressful, keep on persisting through the challenges. Never give up because eventually you will reach your goal, even if it means falling towards it. I want to encourage you to ponder the scripture reading for today; forget what is behind you, and focus on your goal. In the midst of trying times, God is working inside you, and He is making something beautiful of your life. I know it might be painful now, but the end product will be amazing, beautiful, and worthwhile. Don't give up.

ⓩ Reflection

Write down some of your goals for the future. Now write down where things have not succeeded and why you think they have failed. What can you do to move forward? Be deliberate in your thinking; what can you do to keep persisting, even when things don't go the way you planned?

🙏 Prayer

God, give me courage to put the past behind me and to stop checking the rearview mirror. Help me to learn from my failures but embrace this day. I put my trust in You for today. Help me to keep my eye on the goal and realize that my future is in Your hands. I thank You that You know the end from the beginning, and I can trust you with my life. Guide me and lead me in Your way, I pray.

You Are the Guardian
of Your Heart

 Reading: Proverbs 4

Have you ever been in the company of a negative person? Not too pleasant, is it? Their face is usually shrouded in a dark cloud, their voice is laced with bitterness as they spout negativity, and they seem to attract every nasty person within a ten-mile radius. Most negative people have no thought of the well-being of others; their words, like a bludgeon, can batter the soul of the toughest of people. What sad humans, exuding misery, and often blaming others for the state of their heart. There are other people who may say little, but they wallow in their bitterness like a pig in mud. I am not sure which are worse, the silent manipulative people or those spitting venomous words and anger everywhere they go.

Proverbs 4 is an important passage for the health of our soul. Let me make a few observations about this passage.

- You are the caretaker of your heart. No one else is. You are the only person who can guard your heart. Blaming other people for the circumstances of life is never helpful. Don't get into the habit of playing the blame game. You have a choice: to allow a situation to make you bitter and angry, or to make you better and joyful. Take control of your heart, and allow the circumstance you are facing to teach you so that you can learn from the situation. Don't allow yourself to wear the badge of a victim. Viktor Frankl, an Austrian neurologist and writer who survived the horror of the Holocaust, said, "Everything can be taken from a man but one thing: the last of the human freedoms—to choose one's attitude in any given set of circumstances, to choose one's own way." You have a choice before you today, and that is to choose your attitude despite what is going on in your life.

- There is nothing more important than guarding your heart. As Proverbs 4:23 says, "Above all else, guard your heart, for everything you do flows from it." Watching over your heart is a priority. Even though I have been a Christ follower for many years, I still need to be diligent at guarding my attitudes. It is difficult when you have been wronged and people attack or criticize you. But those are not your problems, and there is very little you can do about what other people say or think. What you can do is ensure that you watch your heart, choices, and attitudes in the given circumstance; this alone is your responsibility. The people who harm you must be left in the hands of a loving God, Who cares for their souls as well as yours. That is a safe place to be.

- Everything you do will flow from your heart. If a heart is full of anger and resentment, then that is what will flow from it. The words that proceed from an angry mouth will echo the bitterness of that soul. Negative people can foul the atmosphere of any meeting, and likewise, a happy person can permeate a room with joy.

If your heart is liberated, then grace and beauty will flow from you. When people are internally free, then they live blessed lives and are also a blessing to other people. Encouraging words will flow from a grace-filled heart. I know because I have experienced the beauty of words strung together like beads on a bracelet, bringing beauty and wholeness to my hurting heart.

We have no control over our situation or circumstance. Nor do we have control over what other people do or say. However, we have absolute mastery over our hearts and our attitudes. The habit of daily disciplining our hearts will not only impact us for good but will flow out from our lives and impact others.

Reflection

Write down ways in which you can place safeguards in your heart. Pause and consider what attitudes you have allowed to rule your heart and what you will put in place to guard it.

Prayer

Lord, help me to ensure the health of my heart. Enable me to put grievances behind me so that my soul will be healthy. In all the choices I make throughout the day, help me to be wise. Let goodness and love flow from me to others throughout this day.

The Antidote to Pressure

📖 **Reading: Psalm 46**

Life can be frenetic and demanding. Sometimes, we are so busy rushing from one event to the next that we get to the end of a day feeling frazzled and emotionally drained. That is why most of us feel the need for the weekend or a vacation; we want to get off the carousel of chaos and rest for a while.

I live on the prairie, in the beautiful state of North Dakota. I love to go walking on the plains. There is something very tranquil and peaceful about this monastic space. You can hear the birds sing and listen to the wind whistling through the trees. No screeching cars, no hustle and bustle of city life, just the beauty of God's creation. I do love it when I can stop and listen to the sounds of nature, watch the gentle breeze blowing through the trees making the leaves shiver and tumble onto soft earth. It is in those moments that I feel close to God. Psalm 46:10 says, "Be still and know that I am God." There is something about stillness and quietness that clears our minds, blows out the cobwebs, and makes space for God to speak.

In a world that is filled with pressure, there are ways to restore our souls. Psalm 46 gives me hope when I feel swamped, frazzled, or emotionally exhausted. Those times when anxiety swells in my heart and radiates through my body or when doubts rush in like a flood and wave after wave roll over me, reminding me that I am human, those are the times I pause to let this psalm soak deep into the crevices of my soul and fill me with simple trust in my God. Don't complicate the times of quiet; just learn to sit still.

- Being still helps you to gain a fresh perspective of God. Sitting quietly can give you a deep sense of Who God is. Somehow in the quietness, I am able to grasp the depth and breadth of God's love for me in a way that I cannot do when I am rushing about. Life gets so cluttered with noise that I find I need some space each day for quiet moments to just sit and be. This is not necessarily a time to hear God speaking, but moments where I am still and allow my mind to only think about the Lord. This practice is not easy in the beginning, but the more you discipline your life to a time of quiet in each day, the easier it gets. Being still and quiet is not about what I can get from God; rather, it is about who I become as I sit quietly.

- Being still gives you a fresh perspective on your situation. When I sit quietly or go for a long walk, my problems do not seem as insurmountable as they did in the frantic busyness of life. There are occasions when we need to take time out of our busy schedule to gain a clearer understanding and perspective of our problems. Being still, clearing our minds, and waiting on God can make our situation take on a whole new meaning. Sometimes, sitting still may appear to be a waste of time, and who has time to sit doing nothing? I have learned, however, that the still moments of waiting, and thinking, and reflecting, can save hours of time spent on making a mistake because I was in too much of a hurry.

- Being still gives you a fresh perspective on yourself. When I am still and quiet, I also see myself in a whole new light. There are times I am convinced I cannot handle a situation or accomplish a particular task. But as I sit quietly and draw strength from God, I feel invigorated and confident and able to achieve things I felt I never could. It is not confidence in my own ability but a simple and sure knowledge that God is with me, and He will help me. I gain fresh hope and simple trust. At times, the spiritual side of me gets depleted, and I know in those seasons that I need to give more attention to prayer, reading my Bible, and ensuring I get fellowship with my community. However, when my emotions are expended, I also need to ensure that I take time out to restore and replenish my soul for my own well-being. It is when I am still that I gain a much clearer understanding of myself. In those moments, I gain clarity of what is lacking in my emotional life and gain perspective on myself and my humanity. Being still will help to analyze your soul and secure its well-being.

And so, my friend, as you face this day, I urge you to take a few moments to be quiet. Find time to pause and be alone, or go for a walk where you cannot be distracted, and allow your soul to be still. As you reflect on God and His greatness, you will find courage to face this day with its busyness and pressure.

Reflection

Are you making time to sit quietly and restore your soul? What would be the best time in your day to sit still and fill your mind with God? Now write down how you plan to achieve this goal. Make a commitment to start this practice from today onward.

🙏 Prayer

Lord, I pause in these moments and breathe in Your presence. I sit here quietly, waiting for renewed strength and hope to flow into me to face this day with all its hopes and challenges. Fill me with simple trust to experience the blessing of silence.

Learning to Be Content

📖 **Reading: Philippians 4:6–13**

I have a wonderful mother who is beautiful internally and externally. Her beauty radiates from the inside out, and her smile is contagious. She is deeply loved and appreciated by many people, especially her family. Even in her ninetieth year, grace seems to flow from her like a crystal-clear spring. One of Mom's most outstanding characteristics is her contented heart. Happiness bubbles out of her, whether she is eating her favorite roast dinner or a piece of toast. The other remarkable feature of her life is her gratitude quotient; her score is off the charts. She is thankful for every blessing, and it shows in the way she lives her life. Who wouldn't love a person like that?

The Bible reading today is one we've already looked at, but today, we will focus on a few verses that I will highlight in terms of achieving contentment. So how do we learn contentment? Is it possible to learn to be content? I think so.

- Learning contentment is a discipline. It is interesting to note that Paul says in Philippians 4:12, "I have learned the secret of being content in any and every situation."

He wasn't born with an innate ability; he actually learned or trained himself to be content in every situation he confronted. This is self-discipline. The ability to stop, take stock of yourself, and remind your heart to be thankful. I have already mentioned that I have lived in many different parts of the world. I have also travelled to over fifty different countries. Some of the most contented people I know have very little, and the circumstances of their lives are anything but optimal.

My memories of Africa are often bittersweet. The sights and smells of Africa still linger in my mind. I would walk through the dusty streets of the villages close to where we lived. Little children in their tattered clothes, most of them barefooted, with extended bellies from *kwashiorkor*. Those fortunate to have shoes for their feet were often mismatched and tatty, with barely any soles. I saw mothers carrying heavy buckets of water on their heads, babies strapped to their back, bare and calloused feet kicking up red dust as they made their way back to their simple mud huts, and yet, singing joyously all the way back to their abode. They didn't have much, but those children and their beautiful mothers knew a contentment that some of us in the West, with all our material belongings, know little of. I have never believed that material things make people more contented. Sometimes, stuff may make us more comfortable, but being comfortable and being content are two different things. To be content is a discipline of the heart, and it is something everyone can learn.

• Learning contentment can become a lifestyle. The apostle Paul was probably not naturally inclined to contentment. We read of his previous life as a Jewish man and find that he was a determined, legalistic, hard-nosed Pharisee who set about persecuting anyone who was a Christian. His life certainly did not emanate contentment as he sought to bring destruction to the followers of Jesus. However, when the Lord transformed Paul's life, he became a different person. People who came into contact with him were transformed by his message and the impact of his life. In other words, it was not his preaching alone that affected people, but he influenced them by the way he lived the message he preached. Learning to be content becomes a way of life. When we learn the amazing virtue of being content in every situation, our lives become more meaningful and fulfilled.

I will conclude this devotion with a story about a missionary to India. He wanted to learn to speak the language of the people in his area. A Hindu scholar was recommended to him, and he asked the man if he would assist him in learning the language.

The missionary was taken aback when the Hindu scholar replied, "No, sahib, I cannot teach you my language."

The missionary was confused at the rejection of his request and asked again, "Can you teach me your language? I will pay you for your time."

Once again, the reply came back that he could not teach the missionary his language. When the missionary inquired as to why the scholar could not perform this task, the reply was simple: "No, sahib, I cannot teach you—no man could live with you and not become a Christian."

The consistency and integrity of this missionary's life was so profound that the scholar knew that if he spent time with the man, he would become a Christian. I want to be a Christian like that—to be so authentic that people are impacted by the person I am. Undoubtedly, this missionary exuded a contentment that was contagious.

Reflection

Write down the things that you are content about and the things that are causing discontent. Think about how you can make contentment a lifestyle. Write down three things you will do to channel your life towards contentment.

Prayer

God, help me in my inconsistencies. Enable me to learn the contentment I have read about in Your Word. Whatever my circumstances are, help me to find contentment in every situation of life. May my life and the way I live it bring glory to You today.

The Grass Is Not Greener on the Other Side

 Reading: Psalm 139

Some time ago, I was speaking at a conference in the beautiful country of Ireland. It was one of those crisp, cold, and translucent days when the earth was basking in the lingering rays of the winter sun. There was a lovely pond outside the window, and the reflection of the sun made it sparkle like diamonds. The sun filtered through the windows and filled the room with a soft golden light. As I was winding down to end my talk, I saw the shifting sun and the long shadows cast by the trees and realised the day was quickly fading; the sun dipped behind the horizon. Everything felt so peaceful, so tranquil, almost perfect. I wished in that moment I could simply bask in the beauty of this place and that it would linger a little longer. It really did seem as if the grass was greener in this place. I had just left the cold and dreary Midwest, where nothing looked particularly beautiful at that time of the year.

A young woman came up to me at the close of my session and said, in her broad Irish brogue, "I wish I had your life; it sounds so wonderful." Not many people have said that to me before. I had just been thinking I wished I could stay in this ideal place longer, so she caught me by surprise. From the brief glimpse she had gained of my life, her perception was that mine was better and more exciting than hers. Her limited perspective, and the short sessions I had shared with the women, may have made it appear that my life was perfect, but I assure you my life has been fraught with challenges. Yet I love my life and would not want any other than the one I have right now.

In our reading today, it says that God had each day of my life all mapped out before I was born. I find it comforting to know that God has marked out a journey specifically for me. No other person can run my race because my feet are shod with the shoes the Lord made for me to take this journey. It's easy enough to think the grass is greener on the other side of the fence, but that's a one-sided perspective. Let me encourage you and suggest a few ways to appreciate the grass under your feet.

- Quit looking at the grass on the other side, and appreciate what is under your feet. We can be so obsessed with someone else's good fortune that we fail to stop and see our own. Turn your gaze from other people, and focus on where God has you right now. It may not be the most comfortable place in the world, but it is where He has placed you in this moment. The Psalm in our reading today reveals that He knows everything about us: when we sit and when we rise. What a thought. This omnipotent God is so involved in your life that He knows details as minor as your sitting and rising. God made you, He knows you, and He has placed you right where you are.
- Be thankful for every blade of grass underneath you. It's amazing, but when you learn to be grateful for each blessing that comes your way, it can change your entire perspective on life. When you are constantly comparing

your life with other people, you ignore all the green grass under your feet.

- Remember that God placed you on the grass you are standing on. Appreciate where He has put you; He knows you better than you know yourself. Hebrews 12:1 says, "And let us run with perseverance the race marked out for us." Simply put, God planned your race from the beginning, and as Psalm 139:16 says, "All the days ordained for me were written in your book before one of them came to be." God knew about your today, and He knows about your tomorrow. You can and should feel safe in His plan for your life.

- You will be most comfortable on your own patch of grass. It may look lush and green on the other side of the fence, but truth be told, you will never feel comfortable on someone else's turf. Be content with who you are and where you are.

- Start watering the grass under your feet. Sometimes, we get sidetracked with the grass on the other side of the fence and forget to feed our own grass. Start to nurture your turf, and see how beautiful it begins to look as you care for it instead of wishing for something better.

- As you nourish the grass beneath your feet you will nourish those around you. When you begin to take care of the turf under your feet there will be enough nourishment for you to feed others. I have always found that when my soul is in a good place I can be an encouragement to those around me.

Make a decision to enjoy the day ahead of you. Determine that you will appreciate the grass under your feet and that you will be thankful for where you find yourself. You can be certain of one thing—the great Gardener wants you to flourish on your own patch of grass.

Reflection

Contemplate the ways that God has led you in your journey. If you are not happy with where you are, write down what makes you unhappy. Now write down the things that do make you happy, and determine to concentrate on those things that are positive.

 Prayer

God, thank You for where You have placed me. I want to thank You that every day of my life has been ordained by You. You have numbered my days; help me to live wisely, carefully, and with gratitude for the grass underneath my feet. Help me to have that simple trust and appreciate what I have and not bemoan what I don't have.

Deal Doubt a Death Blow

 Readings: Matthew 14:13–36; Mark 6:30–56

Such a small little word, but what a powerful impact doubt can have on our soul. It can control our thoughts and consequently the way we live our lives. There have been times in my life when I have had grave doubts about my own abilities. Even worse are those occasions when I experienced doubts about the God I love and serve.

I take comfort in the fact that people in the Bible had their doubts as well. Among others, Peter, a disciple of Jesus, had many of those doubt-filled moments. One such incident is recorded in our readings today. Jesus was walking on the water, an event the disciples did not see every day. His followers had seen Him perform the miraculous time and again, but walking on water seemed to take the supernatural to a whole new realm.

I am thankful that the Bible honestly reveals the humanity of people like Peter. He was human, brash, and impulsive, but there was no pretence with him. Peter was obviously flabbergasted at the sight of Jesus walking on water toward the disciples. The Lord encouraged Peter to get out of the boat and walk toward him on the water. Without hesitation, Peter began walking. He was doing well to begin with, but then he turned his head sideways, and his eyes caught a glimpse of the waves. They were big and forceful, and he was immediately overcome with doubt and fear. As those waves rushed towards him, his thoughts would have reinforced the impossibility of a human walking on water, and the moment that doubt invaded his mind, he began to sink, only to have Jesus reach out His hand to save him. Jesus looked at Peter, undoubtedly with compassion, and asked him why he had doubted.

It is easy to be critical of Peter and wonder why he doubted, when Jesus was right there with him in the waves. The simple answer is that he took his eyes off Jesus and looked at the waves. The waves were his focus instead of Jesus.

I have often had to deal with the same kind of doubt that Peter experienced. I have God's Word, I have countless stories of the miraculous, and yet, time and again, I take my eyes off Jesus, and then the circumstances of life come toward me like a wave and threaten to toss me around in doubt. There are times that doubt swirls around and seems to diminish any glimmer of hope. And worse still are the times when it feels as if extinguishing doubt would be like putting out a forest fire with a teacup. If you feel like this today, keep reading.

So how do we deal a death blow to doubt?

- Keep your eyes on Jesus. If you look at the circumstances around you and focus on the wind and the waves, you will begin to doubt. But if you keep your focus on Jesus, the circumstances take on a whole new dimension in light of the God you serve. It is a discipline of heart and mind to keep reminding yourself to concentrate on the promise, not the problem. You might be facing an impossible situation right now. Your own mind has sought resolutions to the problem. Every solution you come up with seems hopeless or impossible. Proverbs 3:5–6 says, "Trust in the Lord with all your heart and lean not on your own understanding; in all your ways submit to him, and he will make your paths straight." Simple trust means that we do not use our human intellect to solve problems. God is infinitely more clever than we are. Even in our wildest imaginings, we cannot conceive how God will solve our problems. So put your trust in Him, and keep your eyes on Jesus.

- Take courage in God. Remind yourself of your humanity, and then affirm the greatness of your God. You are human; you cannot do anything in your own strength, and it is good to admit that you need the help of God to keep doubt from the door. Never give access to doubt when it comes knocking at the portals of your heart. Turn your mind to the greatness of God, and take courage in Him. Yes, people can help you in times of need, but ultimately, you need to draw strength and courage from your God.

- Surround yourself with good people. Belonging to a church is important, but it becomes even more vital to be in fellowship with our church community in those times of doubt and struggle. I can never understand why anyone would stop going to church when the storms of life are brewing all around them. Generally, people do not stop seeing a doctor when their symptoms worsen, but some Christians stop going to church when their doubts intensify and the storm clouds are gathering all around them. Community is exactly what is needed when doubt invades your territory. Make sure that you have some trusted friend in your church family who can support you and pray with you in these times.

- Remind yourself that this season will pass. There are natural cycles of nature, and the same is true of life. Seasons come, and seasons go. I have been through a number of cold, dark seasons in life. There have been times where it felt as if the winter of my soul would linger forever. But just as surely as winter passes and spring comes, so too do those seasons of life come and go. A new day will dawn, and this dismal season will pass. The beauty of transitioning to a new tomorrow is that the dawn of the new season is more magnificent because of the darkness you recently endured.

- Remember that God never changes. Our doubts have nothing to do with the character of God; He is always the same. He never stops loving you or pursuing you. Sometimes, our doubts can change our perception of Jesus. The story in Mark 6:47–50 is telling. The disciples had been with Jesus just a few hours before. They had fed the multitudes and collected twelve basketfuls of leftovers. This was a miracle of mammoth proportions. Some hours later, the disciples see Jesus walking on water, and Mark 6:49 says, "They thought he was a ghost." How strange. They knew Jesus well and had seen His miraculous workings before this occurrence. Now moments later, their perception of Jesus is that He is a "ghost." What was the difference? No, Jesus had not changed. Doubt had altered their perception of who Jesus was. That is what doubt can do. Take courage, my friend; Jesus never changes. He is and always will be Who He says He is. Do not allow doubt to color your perception of God because He is always the same.

Take comfort in a God Who is always there for you. He knows you and understands you better than you do yourself. Peter doubted, and yet Jesus never left him for a moment. He will never leave you, even through your times of doubting. May His grace and peace fill your mind and lift heart and grant you a blessed day.

(symbol) Reflection

Be honest about your doubts, and write them down. Doubting is not a sin, but not asking God for help in times of doubt is foolish. God knows your heart; be honest with Him and let Him know what is in your heart. Reflect on today's reading, and remind yourself of the God you serve.

(symbol) Prayer

God, I do need Your help to live this day. I ask for Your strength to confront the doubts that seem to overshadow my walk with You and at times hold me in their grasp. Give me hope for this day, and enable me to take my eyes off my circumstances and put my simple trust in You.

Seven Reasons to Read the Bible

 Readings: Deuteronomy 6, 2 Timothy 3:16-17

I have always enjoyed reading books. I appreciate the creative ways in which people string words together to tell their stories. Words have power. Some words, like *serendipity*, appear so lively, I can almost see them dancing on the page. Others, like *luscious*, sound delicious, and I can almost taste them. Some words are harsh, cutting, coarse, and raucous, and leave a bitter taste in my mouth. Then there are boring, drab words that need other words to give them some color; yes, words are powerful.

When I read my Bible, every one of those feelings I have described impinge on me. The Bible is colourful, honest, gruesome, bloody, and beautiful, all at the same time.

I have been touched by bibliographies, challenged by all genres of Christian literature, informed by history, awed by science, and stirred by poetry. Of all the books I have ever read, none has ever touched my soul more deeply or profoundly than the Bible.

Here are seven reasons to read the Bible:

- The Bible inspires. I have read the Bible more times than I can remember, but I never grow tired of it. I am inspired by the contrasting and varied stories therein, some sad, others gruesome, and many victorious. No matter how often I read about Joseph, I see something new each time I return to that story, and every time I read it, I am inspired to live more intentionally. My faith is regularly enlarged as the truth of God's Word settles in my soul.
- The Bible challenges. When I read the stories of the lives of Jesus and His disciples, I am challenged to live a holy life. I cannot read the Bible without it confronting my commitment to Jesus. Whenever I've been filled with fear about a new venture I am undertaking, I have been challenged by Gideon or Moses or Nehemiah to step out in courage, as they did. If it were not for the Bible and its challenging impact on me, I would never have undertaken many opportunities.
- The Bible convicts. I grew up in the city of Johannesburg, South Africa. My family were nominal Christians who went to church most Sundays. I recall a sultry, hot day in January 1969, when I was thirteen years old, listening to some young people speaking about how God had transformed their lives. They read several verses from the Bible, which convicted me and spoke to my heart. My response was to open my heart and life to a God Who loved me and had a far better plan for my life than I did.

I made that decision five decades ago, and it is one I have never regretted. To this day, I find the Bible still speaks to my soul. Whenever I stray from the right path, the Bible convicts me and shows me a better way to live. That is why I am disciplined to read my Bible every day. I want God to speak to me through His Word and challenge be about my failings and flaws so I can walk in step with Him.

- The Bible encourages. Whenever I feel discouraged, God's Word encourages my heart. In some of the most challenging hours of my life, the Bible has been my deepest comfort and strength; it has been my anchor through many storms. No other volume in the world has given me more encouragement than this amazing book we call the Bible. I recall the day a policeman came to my front door to tell me that Jason, our son, had been in a horrendous car accident. Immediately, a verse of the Bible sprang to my mind: "All the days ordained for me were written in your book before one of them came to be" (Psalm 139:16). That portion of the Bible gave me immense courage to face the gruelling weeks ahead of me (the next devotion describes how he came through this ordeal).
- The Bible sustains. Reading God's Word sustains me as a Christ follower. I want to be a healthy and strong Christian, and the only way to sustain my commitment to Jesus is to go to His Word on a daily basis. I find when my devotional life slips, everything begins to slide.
- The Bible guides. Yes, I find guidance for my daily life by reading the Bible. When I need direction, I get on my knees and pray. I find God speaks to my heart through His Word, and He guides me and directs my path.
- The Bible strengthens. The more I read my Bible, the stronger I grow in my faith and in my commitment to Jesus. I want to be strong so that when challenges and difficulties come, I can withstand them. The Bible strengthens me for today, but it also fortifies me for my tomorrow.

I know too many people who fluctuate in their devotional life. They read the Bible sporadically and only go to God's Word if they have a problem. If you want to be strong in your faith, you need to make reading your Bible a daily habit. Don't let your Bible reading be a chore or something to get over and done with. Read God's Word so you will be inspired, challenged, encouraged, and all the other reasons I mentioned. The final benefit to reading the Bible is that you get your heart in earshot of God and what He wants to say through His Word.

 ## Reflection

Write down ways in which the Bible has helped you in your daily life. Now express on paper how you can enhance your daily reading. Write down your goals for the next month, and determine what you want to accomplish in your daily Bible reading.

 ## Prayer

God, thank You for the Bible. Help me to hear You speaking to my heart through Your word. Guide me and lead me so that I can make wise decisions and live my life carefully and thoughtfully. Let Your Word fill my mind and my heart throughout this day.

The Purpose of Pain

 Reading: Psalm 30

I hate pain. Any kind of pain is awful. Physical pain can be debilitating, but there is something about an inner ache that can be far worse. The pain I am referring to is emotional pain, or what we often call heartache. If you are reading this devotional, then you have experienced some type of internal pain. You may have experienced more heartache than you thought possible. And the question shouting out amid all that pain, demanding an answer, is, What is the purpose of pain? This is a fair question, but there is no easy answer.

As I contemplated this devotional, I did a fair bit of internalising. I found myself going down the corridors of my mind, picking off scabs and opening old wounds as I searched to find meaning in my pain. In many ways, it has been a painful process as memories, some happy and others not, have come to the surface again.

I do believe that memory is a gift. It allows us to reflect on the past and make wise choices for the future. One moment it fills our hearts with warmth and the next with sadness. Even painful memories serve a purpose in our lives because without them, we would be less than human.

As I reflected on my pain, let me share my thoughts with you:

- Pain is not a normal state. A life filled with continual pain is not the norm, and I don't believe God ever intended it to be so. However, there are times when pain does serve a purpose. Pain reveals that something is wrong, and because of that, we have to respond in some way or other. Responding to pain is human. Your first response may be anger or tears or regret or sorrow. That is a normal and natural response because it expresses your humanity. Holding pain in and not allowing some type of release is not good for your physical or mental well-being. Do not try to be brave; allow your broken heart release. Releasing your emotions is not weakness; it is human. Most of all, allow God to walk with you through your pain and suffering.
- God is always with us in our pain. When Jay had his terrible car accident (written about in my memoir, *Wild Hope*), I went through the darkest hours of my existence, as his sick and broken body hovered on the brink of death. I felt as if the angel of death was sitting right there, waiting to snatch him up in his ugly grasp. I have never felt such desperation. But God was there in my pain, revealing His love through people, friends, our church community, and family from all around the world. In those dark moments, God displayed His love to me in the most remarkable ways. It did not ease the pain, but I look back in the rearview mirror of my mind and see His fingerprints in every detail of that awful time. Don't push God away when you are in pain; allow Him to walk with you through your dark night.
- Pain reveals our humanity and capacity for love. I would never have known the internal pain for my son if I had not experienced the intense love I had for him. Blaise Pascal

put it this way "If you do not love too much, you do not love enough." It is because I loved so deeply that I grieved so profoundly. And in that sense, pain is a gift because if I had not known love, I would never have known this pain. Truth be told, my life is richer because of my ability to love so deeply. Can you imagine not feeling pain when there is loss? My pain exposes my humanity and my capacity to love. If I never knew pain, then I'd never know love. My humanity would be diminished without love and pain.

- Pain teaches us lessons we could never have learned elsewhere. I learned that life is short and the people I love can be snatched away in a moment. When I was young, my dad always said to me, "Life can change in a split-second." How true it is that one second can change our lives forever.

  Our days are numbered, and truth be told, none of us know when it's time to breathe our final breath. Because of what we went through with Jay's accident, our family has learned to value each moment we have with each other. We don't think you can ever say, "I love you" enough. Each moment with one another other is an extraordinary gift that we treasure. In our family, there will always be an echo of joy emanating from a memory of deep pain. Pain taught me to cherish each moment.

- Go through pain with grace. People are watching you in your pain. The world and the church are desperate for people who model suffering well. I well remember our long nightmare in the Trauma Intensive Care Unit of North Carolina's Medical Centre. Through the pain, we lived out our faith during that time. Many people visiting their loved ones in that ward would ask us to come and pray for them. We had amazing opportunities to share our faith with the health care workers as well. I recall one nurse saying to Paul, "Thank you." He asked why she was thanking him because we were so filled with gratitude for all the medical staff were doing for Jay. She said, "Since you have been in this ward, our records show people are getting better quicker. And the staff here are all getting along so much better since the Alexanders came into this ward." It was a humbling moment, but we were grateful that our faith was able to impact others during a time of our personal agony and trial.

If your heart is aching, and you wonder if you'll ever smile again, be assured that the darkness will pass, and the sun will shine again. The Bible assures us, "Weeping may stay for the night, but rejoicing comes in the morning" (Psalm 30:5). Your morning will come, but until then, allow God to hold your hand and see you through this season. The Psalm in our devotion today ends by saying, "You turned my wailing into dancing; you removed my sackcloth and clothed me with joy, that my heart may sing your praises and not be silent. Lord my God, I will praise you forever" (Psalm 30:11–12). Coming through this time of heartache and pain leaves the psalmist with an emotion so strong that he can only conclude by saying he will never stop praising his God.

Whether your pain is from a broken relationship, the death of a loved one, a difficult marriage, or a child gone astray, God will uphold you. The intensity of your pain will pass, the dawn will come, and when the sun rises, I assure you its beauty will be more astounding because of the darkness of your night. Be blessed; you are special, and God loves you.

(⟲) Reflection

Write in as many sentences as you need the pain you are experiencing. Speak to God, and let Him know what is in your heart. Have you shared your pain with a trusted friend who can pray for you? Ask God to reveal someone who can hold your hand through this dark night.

Prayer

God, I need Your help with my pain. Take my hand and walk with me through this valley. Please let me hold on fast and put my simple trust in You. I know and believe this season will pass and a new day will dawn, but until then, uphold me with Your righteous hand.

Dealing with the Shadows of the Past

 Reading: Philippians 3:1-14

I was sitting outside on a deck chair, listening to the birds chirping and feeling the breeze blowing through the trees, when a memory from the past flooded my thoughts. I am not sure if it was the smell of the damp earth, the song of the birds, or the warmth of the sun, but those memories surfaced with crystal clarity.

I am sure that like me, many of you have experienced those moments when a smell, sight, or sound triggered a memory from the past. You may have thought that those memories had long been buried, but they were lurking in the corners of your mind and pushed their way to the surface, making you feel happy, sad, regretful, or hurt. We now return to a passage we previously considered, but I want to cast a different light on it. The apostle Paul urges us in our walk, "Forgetting what is behind and straining toward what is ahead, I press on toward the goal to win the prize for which God has called me heavenward in Christ Jesus" (Philippians 3:13–14). Paul is not asking us to ignore the past but to deal with it.

All of us have a story to tell. We can share our triumphs and our tragedies, and perhaps we feel as if there were fewer victories along the road. Memories can open wounds from our past that we thought had healed, whereas other memories can fill us with joy. Whatever the case, I am glad that we can go back into our memory box and draw out of our experiences, good or bad. Memories are important and vital to our overall health and well-being.

How do we deal with our memories? How do we move on from the shadows of our past and find healing or forgiveness for today? Here are a few thoughts that might be helpful:

- We can learn valuable lessons from the shadows of our past. I don't like dwelling on my failures, and I certainly don't enjoy thinking about the people who have deliberately tried to hurt me. However, I can honestly say that as I look back at those shadows in my life, I have learned more from the dark periods than any of my joy-filled experiences. Once I learn the lesson, I need to move on from my past and not keep checking my rearview mirror. This is what Paul means when he says that we should forget what happened in our past; he is not encouraging you to pretend your past is unimportant but telling you to move on from it.

- We can grow stronger through the shadows of our past. We fall, but we get up again. Yes, we strive to be more cautious because we have learned a bit of wisdom along the way. Actually, the truth is that we still fall and fail, but we rise up and gain strength. The experiences of life toughen us up; they give us courage and determination and strength to keep going, even when we don't want to.

- We can develop empathy for other people because of the shadows of our past. We can feel other people's pain because we know the agony they are experiencing. We would never be able to really help others if we didn't have shadows from our past that we had to work through to attain victory. The most empathetic people I know are those who have fallen down, got wounded, and yet, got up again, dusted themselves off, and moved on. I know that my experiences have given me a compassion for people in distress that I would never have had if I had not gone through some dark valleys.

- We are where we are today because of the shadows of the past. I didn't enjoy the pain and hurt I have known. Some of it was of my own making, and some was not. There have been injustices that I've had to bear, and it has not been easy. Strange as this may sound, I am grateful for the path I have taken and the lessons I have learned through my pain. I have made some stupid mistakes that I lived to regret. I have said things I should never have said. I have also been hurt, chosen to forgive, and been healed. I have failed people, and people have failed me, but I have learned to trust again and tried to be a better person who can also be trusted. I know that I am where I am right now because of all I have gone through.

- We don't linger in the shadows; we move into the light of a new day. That is the ultimate goal that the apostle Paul urged us onto. You will never achieve your goal if you remain living in the shadows of your past. Move out of the clouds into the light of this new day.

The darkness of your past is there to remind you that you have more resilience than you thought. It not there to hold you back, but to enable you to move into your future. Make today the first day of the rest of your life. Don't let the shadows of yesterday hold you back; rather, let them lead you to a new day.

Reflection

Write down some of the shadows of your past that still linger in the corners of your mind. What have you learned from those experiences? How can you move beyond the darkness into the future God has for you?

 Prayer

God, thank You for my memory and the ability to reflect on the good and the bad. Thank You that the shadows of my past can now become the path to a good future because I am growing wiser and learning to reflect on my failures and learn through them. Help me to stay humble and teachable, and to grow in simple trust.

How to Deal with Anger

 Reading: Ephesians 4:26–32

In the darkness of the night, you toss and turn in your bed. As the mauve and amber shades tint the skies in the early-morning hours, you continue wrestling with your thoughts. It feels as if not only your sheets are strangling you but so are your thoughts. And the culprit for your restlessness is a five-letter word: anger. There may be stillness in the night, but the noise inside your soul is thumping through your entire being.

Did you know that the Bible deals with this topic? Yes, because people who loved God also experienced anger. I have been angry many times in my life. Sometimes, that anger was justifiable. But there have also been times that I have fuelled my anger by dwelling on the issue and mulling it over and over until it almost got to the brink of allowing bitterness to invade my heart. When I realized how close I was to the destructive emotion of bitterness, I went to the Lord with my problem.

Let me make a few comments about anger.

- Anger is not always sinful. God wired us with all kinds of emotions, and we all react to circumstances and situations differently. We always respond to our emotions in some way or another. Feeling and experiencing anger is not wrong; it is human, but how we deal with this emotion is essential to the well-being of our soul. Ephesians 4:26 exhorts us, "In your anger do not sin." In other words, you can be angry with a right heart, or alternatively, you can let your anger lead you to sin.

- Anger must be managed carefully. Anger has filled my heart many times and for various reasons. I have to admit there are times I get angry about the slide in morality within our culture. It grieves my spirit because I am concerned for the young people who are navigating the moral ambiguity in today's society. I have felt anger about the decisions some political leaders make because I know their choices are not for the well-being of others, but solely for their own political agenda. So I do get angry. But I try not to allow those issues to dominate my thinking. I pray about them and then intentionally move on. I cannot allow anger to fester in my spirit; it won't do me any good, and it certainly does not help the situation. You can be angry, but you must not allow that anger to control you. You need to ensure that you are always in control of your emotions.

    Getting angry with family and the people closest to us is another issue. Because we are close to these people, and we love them, other emotions can get in the way. We must never allow our anger to get in the middle of our relationships and cause them harm. Managing anger in a careful, deliberate, and strategic way is vital for our souls. Proverbs 29:11 says, "Fools give full vent to their rage, but the wise bring calm in the end." Your goal should always be to resolve a situation in as peaceful a way as possible. Don't allow anger to linger in your soul. Confront the issue that caused the anger so that it does not damage a relationship long term.

- Anger must be confronted. Ephesians 4:26 says, "Do not let the sun go down while you are still angry, and do not give the devil a foothold." Never go to bed with an angry heart. This is wise advice because stewing over an issue is not going to help you sleep, and furthermore, it is not good for your overall health and well-being. Confront your anger. If you can, you should speak to the person who has made you angry. Sometimes, hearing their perspective can help you see the situation in a whole new light. If it is not possible to have a talk with the person who has inflamed your anger, then pray about the situation. You must try to do something constructive, even if it means speaking to a trusted friend and asking them for prayer support. If you do not deal with your anger, I can almost guarantee that it will be destructive in the long term. Perpetual anger is not good for your soul or your long-term health.

  Psychological research has shown the link between our emotional health and our physical well-being. Anger is one of those emotions that can whittle away at our physical wellness. The Bible spoke about the link between emotional and physical well-being long before psychologists discovered this connection. Proverbs 17:22 says, "A cheerful heart is good medicine, but a crushed spirit dries up the bones." I assure you that anger will dispel any joy from your heart, and continual anger will deplete your soul.

The word *sorry* can go a long way. There are times we need to express this word, and other times, we need to hear it. We are not responsible for the actions of other people or their words. If they do not apologize, that is not your problem. Never make someone else's problem yours. You have to ensure that your heart is right, and if your conscience is clear, then that is all that matters.

Reflection

Write down the reasons for the anger you feel. Is your anger justified, or have you allowed it to linger so long that it is now out of proportion? How are you dealing with those feelings? What can you do to diminish the anger and feel the peace that only God can give? Is there someone you need to confront? Write their name down and pray for them and then determine to resolve the issue in some way.

Prayer

God, I pray for Your help in dealing with my anger. I do not want it to control every aspect of my life. Help me to take the necessary steps to resolve this situation, and put my heart at rest, knowing that You will work in the midst of my circumstances.

Waiting for God's Will and His Time

 Reading: 1 Kings 17

I am not an innately patient person. This elusive virtue has often lacked in my life. My daughter, Anna, has been graced with a beautiful disposition, and one of her enviable traits is her persistent patience, which I assure you she did not inherit from me. I do not like waiting for things to happen, for situations to improve, or for projects to be completed. Truth be told, I really do not like waiting for anything. If I had my way, I would forge ahead with every opportunity and would probably run ahead of myself and God, if I could. But I can't, which is a good thing.

Throughout my years of serving the Lord, He has taught me patience. It has been a long and hard lesson, but I am thankful for the patience God has displayed with me, His stubborn child. Believe me, patience is not an easy lesson for an impatient person to learn.

I love the story of Elijah in our reading today. If you read 1 Kings 17:1–10, you will see a man who sat patiently waiting for the Lord. It was only when God spoke to Elijah that he moved. So what are some of the lessons we can learn from this prophet?

- Don't do anything until God speaks. I can hear you saying, "How do I know when God is speaking?" Well, if you are still and quiet, and your heart is in earshot of God, He will speak to you. Sometimes, we hear God through our daily reading of the Bible; other times, it is just a sense of peace in your heart after you prayed about a situation. And at other times, it can be a prompt or a nudge that God gives you through a sermon or a word spoken through someone else. Elijah sat quietly at the brook of Kerith and waited until God spoke to him. Only when he heard God's voice did he move on to the next place.

  If you read further in 1 Kings 19:3, you see a somewhat different picture of Elijah. He is running from Jezebel, the wicked, corrupt queen of Israel, because he is afraid. A little farther on in the passage, it says, "There he went into a cave and spent the night. And the word of the Lord came to him: 'What are you doing here, Elijah?'" (1 Kings 19:9). Elijah had moved out of fear and not out of obedience, and God asked him why he moved. That is a dangerous place to be. He had not waited to hear from God but had responded to his own fear by running away. We should ensure that we never move out of fear, anger, failure, resentment, or any other reason. It is important to take the next step because we know it is God's will for our lives.

- The will of God is the safest place on earth. It may not always be the most comfortable place, and it may not be the place you would have chosen to be, but it will be a safe place. When Elijah went to Zarephath, it was extremely dangerous from a human perspective. This was a foreign place, and Jezebel (his enemy) was from Zarephath. I know if I wanted to hide from my foe, I wouldn't choose to cower in the land they were living. Add to all these challenges the fact that the people of Zarephath were Baal worshipers. Wouldn't you want to get as far away from them as you possibly could? The point is, Zarephath was God's will for Elijah, and so it was the right place to be. And because it was the appropriate place from God's perspective, it was also a safe place. It may not have been the most beautiful, tranquil, or prosperous city, but it was exactly where God wanted Elijah.

- God works in our hearts in the waiting period. We may be impatient and want to move, but the truth is, God knows when we are ready. He is always working in our hearts during the waiting period. I am not sure how long Elijah waited at Zarephath—three years or more? I do know that while he was there, God was preparing his heart for the next step, which you read about in 1 Kings 18. Without Zarephath, there would not have been a victorious Mount Carmel experience. Some of the difficult places in my life have also been preparation for the next step God had for me.

I encourage you to wait patiently. God has a plan for your life. Sit quietly, and allow Him to work in your heart during this waiting period. He is preparing you for something unique and special. If you want a Carmel experience, you need a place like Zarephath first.

Reflection

Tell God what you are waiting for. Write down what you want Him to do inside of you in this period of waiting. Pray that the Lord will give you the patience to wait for His perfect time.

🙏 Prayer

God, I want Your will in my life more than my own. I pray for the virtue of patience today because I have felt it eluding me of late. Help me to attune my ear to Your voice that I may be assured of Your direction. Give me that simple trust in this time of waiting.

Can the Bible Be Trusted?

 Readings: 2 Timothy 2:15–26; Joshua 1:7–9

Can the Bible be trusted? Wow; what a question. But it's one that I believe should be asked. And Christians should be willing to look for answers. We need never be afraid of what we might find because the Bible will always stand the test of time.

It is true that people have tried to discredit the authenticity of the Bible and even deny the existence of a Creator. The renowned scientist Richard Dawkins argues that the Bible is a myth and that God isn't real. In his book *God Delusion,* Dawkins states that a supernatural creator almost certainly does not exist and that religious faith is a delusion. He pushes his argument further by adding that evolution is one of the most solid theories in science.

The brilliant scientist Stephen Hawking, who died in 2018, admitted to being an atheist, arguing that science offers a "more convincing explanation" because in his view, the origins of the universe and the miracles of religion "aren't compatible" with scientific fact.

No one could deny the intelligence of these two men, but there are countless clever scientists all over the world who claim that God is Creator and that His Word, the Bible, is trustworthy.

Scientists throughout the centuries have attested to the authenticity of scripture. Men such as Copernicus, Descartes, Newton, and Einstein had no conflict with the compatibility of science and the Bible. There are scientists today who also affirm the Bible and worship God.

I am being simplistic here, but let me make a few comments after doing some study of my own (remember that there is a limit to what I can say in a devotional):

- The historical reliability of the Bible has been confirmed. It is ludicrous to suggest that people who believe in the validity of the Bible are nonscientific and blindly follow what they read. Christian historians, theologians, and scientists have studied the Bible and have not been afraid to subject it to the same scrutiny as they would any other ancient manuscript.

- Sound methods have been used to analyze ancient biblical documents: Historians have assessed manuscripts from all around the Mediterranean—Egypt, Syria, Turkey, Greece—and have been able to reconstruct the original text with about 99.5 percent accuracy. There is no evidence that New Testament books were doctored or that material was added. Time and space limit me from elaborating on this subject, but I am confident enough to urge you to study further and explore for yourself. I know that God's book will stand up to the test.

- Other ancient texts. Did you know that we have fourteen thousand fragments of the New Testament, and many of those dating from a few decades after they were first written? When it comes to Plato and Aristotle, we have only a few copies, and the time gap between the original and existing documents is much longer. I never hear anyone question the authenticity of the books of either of these two men.

This is a brief glimpse into the reliability of the Bible and hopefully an encouragement to those who read it. If you have doubts, do your own research; your heart and mind will take courage in the evidence that is out there to prove the authenticity of the Bible.

I know what the Bible means to me. It is the one book I have read that always convicts me, stirs my heart, and challenges me to change. No book in the world touches my heart like the Bible. That may not be proof to anyone else, but my heart says a quiet and resounding "Thank you, Lord; I know you are real." I believe the Bible is authentic because it has been tried and tested. I know that it is reliable because no book has impacted lives more lastingly and significantly than the Bible. I understand this is merely anecdotal evidence, but it affirms what has been tried and tested.

My prayer is that you will open the Bible and allow it to speak to your heart. It has been speaking to hearts through the centuries, and God still uses His Word to challenge and change hearts in this complicated and challenging twenty-first century.

Reflection

If you have doubts about the authenticity of the Bible, write them down. What can you read or study to know and understand the Bible better? What can you do to test the validity of the Bible?

Prayer

God, thank You for the Bible. Help me to study Your Word diligently and to ask the difficult questions. Guide me, and lead me step by step. Above all else, help me to embody what I read and live out the message of this amazing book You have given Your people.

Why Do Bad Things Happen to Good People?

 Reading: John 16

Life is full of mysteries, and suffering and pain are two of them. There are questions that hang in the air like an unfinished sentence. Why did God allow this tragedy? What kind of God would allow this awful sickness? At times, there are situations and circumstances that make absolutely no sense, or so it seems from our perspective.

The question that many have puzzled over is, Why do bad things happen to good people? And I suppose it is a fair question. Job asked that question, and so do many of the psalms. People ask that question when there is a tragedy, an earthquake, a war, or a famine. I have pondered this question, and although I do not have all the answers, I do think that the Bible can help. Jesus always told the truth, unlike some religious leaders who try to fob off pain and suffering. John 16:33 says, "I have told you these things, so that in me you may have peace. In this world you will have trouble. But take heart! I have overcome the world." We live in an imperfect world, and because of that reality, we will experience pain and suffering. Bad things do happen to good people; Jesus addressed this issue in Luke 13:4–5. Let's consider what the Bible has to say about this topic.

- God did not create a world of pain and suffering. Genesis 1:31 says, "God saw all that he had made, and it was very good." God made a wonderful and a good world that was later corrupted by the sin of man. There is a suffering that comes from our own moral choices. Some of our suffering can be the result of our action (or inaction).

  Many wars have been fought because of evil and immoral leaders. They have caused untold suffering to thousands because of their greed and lust for power and control. God gave us free will, and unfortunately, some have used their free will in a corrupt and abusive way. Many people suffer hunger on a daily basis. How can we blame God for this? The world produces enough food to feed everyone, and yet still, many go hungry. Once again, it is an abuse of wealth and power.

- God can bring good out of suffering. Romans 8:28 says, "And we know that in all things God works for the good of those who love him, who have been called according to his purpose." God doesn't create suffering and pain, but He can bring good out of our pain. I have seen people go through incredible suffering and come through it in a remarkable way. They have been able to use their pain to help others in difficulty. I know that the painful experiences of my life shaped me and made me more compassionate and caring for the needs of other people.

  Consider the story of Joseph in Genesis 37–50. He suffered grave injustice on many counts. His jealous brothers threw him into a pit and left him to die, but God sent men to rescue him. He was brought to Potiphar's house and served him faithfully and diligently. When Joseph withdrew from the advances of Potiphar's wife, she falsely accused him, and he was thrown into prison. The injustice was almost palpable. In prison, he found favour and once again served diligently; God used all these experiences to not only deliver and promote Joseph, but to rescue a nation. There was purpose to Joseph's suffering, and if we are God's children, He works even in our suffering and pain to bring something good. 1 Peter 5:10 says, "And the God of all grace, who called you to his eternal glory in Christ, after you have suffered a little while, will himself restore you and make you strong, firm and steadfast." That is a promise worth remembering.

- All Christians will suffer. The Bible says we will experience trouble in this world. Paul's theology also encapsulates cross-bearing suffering for those who love God. We live in the world and are subject to the laws of the universe. Things will go wrong because bad things happen to good and bad people alike. Suffering is par for the course. When there is a natural disaster, good and bad suffer together. Some natural disasters occur because of human stupidity. At times, we have not cared for the environment as we should, and consequently, natural disasters occur, and when they do, all suffer alike. However, there are times that suffering can also be the result of our own foolish decisions, and yet, even in those situations, God is there to pick us up.

- God will bring suffering to an end. One day, all suffering will cease. That will be a wonderful day, and in the light of eternity, everything will pale in comparison. God is a good God. He does not get some morbid pleasure in watching His children suffer. Hardships will come, as we read in 2 Timothy 3:12: "In fact, everyone who wants to live a godly life in Christ Jesus will be persecuted." We will indeed suffer whether we are good or bad. But take heart in what John says in Revelation 21:4: "He will wipe every tear from their eyes. There will be no more death or mourning or crying or pain, for the old order of things has passed away." My friend, that day is coming when all suffering, pain, and heartache will end.

Every person will go through pain and suffering, to varying degrees. We are not exempt from pain and heartache because we are Christians. The wonderful truth is that Jesus bears our suffering with us. We do not go through our pain alone. He will walk with us through every trial, if we allow Him. We live in an imperfect world, and because of that, we are not exempt from suffering. We are exposed to the same moral and natural forces as everyone else, and we pay the price for the decisions we make, and unfortunately, we pay a price for some of the decisions the powerful and elite make. God gave us free will, and we live with the consequences of our choices. I believe it is up to each person to make good choices so that our world will be a better place. We should ensure, as far as possible, that our choices never cause other people harm.

⏳ Reflection

Pause and write about an experience that has caused suffering in your life. Does it feel unfair? Why? Ask God for the grace to go through this period and enable you to learn from it.

🙏 Prayer

Lord, my circumstances seem out of control, but I remind myself that You are in complete control. I look for Your sustaining grace and comfort in this time. I know that You are working inside of me, even though I am hurting, and it feels as if You are far away. I ask You to hold me tight and to see me through. I cling to the promise that You work all things together for good.

Dealing a Decisive Blow
to Negativity

 Reading: Numbers 13–14

I love being around positive people because they inspire and energize me. And I must be honest and say that I find negative people draining and exhausting. Have you noticed that you don't see any seminar advertisements for "How to Grow Your Negativity Quotient"? Truth be told, most of us are prone to negativity and need help being positive.

I constantly challenge myself with putting away negative thoughts; they seem to slip through the back door of my mind with ease, and those thoughts can be stubborn. At times, they tenaciously hold onto my brain. I know that I have to take these thoughts captive before they take control.

Numbers 13 is a chapter I have visited many times in my Christian life. It is the sad story of twelve spies who go and investigate the land of Canaan. When they get back from their expedition, they give Moses a negative and bad report of their findings. Their negativity cost them everything. That particular generation of people never entered the Promised Land, apart from

Joshua and Caleb—the only two who went back to Moses with a positive story about the land.

If you are anything like me, you want to beat this negativity syndrome. So how do we do this? There are three simple principles you need to apply to your life:

- Challenge your thought life. In my negative moments, a molehill can seem like a mountain. When we are negative, our perspective on most things is colored by our bad attitude. The only way to deal with it is to be honest with ourselves and challenge our thinking. Get an accountability partner if you need to and ask them to challenge you whenever you speak negatively. Someone once said, "Sow a thought and you reap an act. Sow an act and you reap a habit. Sow a habit and you reap a character. Sow a character and you reap a destiny." Who we are and what we eventually become begins with a thought. If we do not learn to control our thoughts and ensure that they are wholesome, our entire lives and future will be impacted by those thoughts. If you think negatively, then it stands to reason that you will act in the same manner. Our thoughts are powerful, and that is why we need to control them.

- Change your thought life. Sometimes, it is necessary to reprogram your brain. In other words, you need to sew new thoughts into the fabric of your mind. Romans 12:2 says, "But be transformed by the renewing of your mind." If you want to change your thought life, then you need to be deliberate and intentional about doing so. Start your day by talking to God and reading His Word. Every time a negative thought comes into your mind, stop, challenge that thought, and say a Bible verse out loud if you can (if not, you can say it silently, over and over). The point is that if you want to change your thinking, you need to be deliberate and work diligently at this discipline.

- Choose positive words. You may be in the habit of responding in a particular way to people. For example, when someone asks how you are, you may reply, "Not too bad." Think about those words; they are not sinful, but neither are they positive. Consider the words you speak. When you say you are not too bad, you are also saying that you are not too good. That is negative. Think about the blessings of another new day, that you are alive and have food and clothing. Your language should reflect gratitude. So even if you are not feeling wonderful, you can still say, "I am thankful to be alive" or "It's a beautiful day, and I am grateful." If you want to change your thought patterns, then start changing your speech. Many times, our words can be far more destructive than this simple example, so it is in our best interest to watch our vocabulary to ensure that wholesome and positive words come from our lips.

Negative people are not happy; usually, they are determined to make other people's lives miserable as well. I know we don't live in a perfect world, and I understand that things don't always go our way, but we live in a world where God has made Himself known to us. We are surrounded by His creation. And above all else, He loves us. Start your day with gratitude to God for a new day. Be deliberate in thinking and speaking out the blessings in your life. This can put a whole new perspective on your circumstances and can turn a seemingly negative day into an extraordinary one.

Let us wage war on negativity in our minds and in our world. I trust that your life will reflect the radiance of your God, Who is all-powerful and all positive. Make a choice to beat negativity.

Reflection

Write down the negative thoughts that play over in your mind. What are you going to do to deal a decisive blow to negative thoughts that keep pervading your mind? Write down one meaningful scripture verse you can memorize to help you when negative thoughts push their way into your brain.

Prayer

God, I am so thankful for a new day. Another day to breathe Your air and delight in Your creation. Help me to pause throughout the day to count my blessings. Give me the strength I need to put any and every negative thought from my mind.

Watching Our Words

 Readings: Proverbs 10; James 3

I have done a lot of thinking about the power of the tongue. Not only because words have hurt me and offended me, but because I know that I have said hurtful words to others. The book of James says the tongue is the smallest member of the body, yet it can cause the greatest devastation. Have you ever said anything that you wished you could take back? As the words left your mouth, you regretted what you said. I have often wished I could swallow the words that tumbled out of my mouth in a moment of anger or thoughtlessness. Unfortunately, you can't take your spoken words back. I have already alluded to the power of words, and in our previous devotion, I said, "Choose positive words." I know how important it is to watch our words.

Many years ago, I heard the story of a man who was sick in hospital. He had a colleague who came to see him to apologize for some unkind and harsh things he had said about him. His colleague sat on his hospital bed and said, "Can you forgive me for the terrible things I said about you?" The sick man said he could and he would certainly forgive his colleague. But then he made an unusual request.

He said to his colleague, "Won't you take my pillow and open the zipper and then go to the window, open it, and shake all the feathers outside?"

The man thought it was a rather odd request but obliged the sick man he had offended.

The ailing man then made another unusual request: "Now will you go and gather all those feathers up again?"

The gentleman who had shaken the feathers out of the window replied in an astounded tone, "That is impossible; by now, the feathers will have blown all over the town."

The sick man responded: "Exactly," and then continued, "And that is precisely what has happened with your words; they are all over town now. They have damaged my reputation; you are sorry, I forgive you, but the destructive force of your words has done great harm."

That is a sobering truth. Once those words are out of your mouth, they have caused damage and hurt. Of course, that doesn't absolve you from apologising, but it should make you think carefully about the words that proceed from your mouth in the future.

There are some things we need to consider about our words:

- The tongue has great power. Our tongues have the power to do harm or bring healing. Psalm 141:3 says, "Set a guard over my mouth, Lord: Keep watch over the door of my lips." The psalmist acknowledges his humanity and asks the Lord to help him. He wants to be deliberate about watching his words. We understand our weakness and know how prone we are to say things we should never say. So with intentionality, we ask God to help us to speak kindly and lovingly so that our words will bring life and not destruction.

  Let's take a few moments to reflect on the chapter we read in Proverbs. I love the picture the writer paints for us with his pen. He says, "The mouth of the righteous is a fountain of life, but the mouth of the wicked conceals violence" (Proverbs 10:11). The writer contrasts the words of a good person and those of an evil person. He augments his thoughts, adding, "Wisdom is found on the lips of the discerning, but a rod is for the back of one who has no sense" (Proverbs 10:13). We are left in no doubt here that unwise people will pay for their stupidity. Read further; Proverbs 10:19 says, "Sin is not ended by multiplying words, but the prudent hold their tongues." Wise people can control what proceeds from their lips, and in stark contrast, foolish people just multiply their foolishness by not knowing when to be silent. Proverbs 10:20 says, "The tongue of the righteous is choice silver, but the heart of the wicked is of little value." How graphic the contrast between the words of the wise and the foolish. Jesus said something similar: "For the mouth speaks what the heart is full of" (Matthew 12:34). Again, we read in Proverbs 10:21, "The lips of the righteous nourish many, but fools die for lack of sense." What an amazing contrast there is to the words of the wise and the foolish. If our words are wise, then they can nourish other people. Simply put, our words become life giving to others. Just as food can sustain the hungry person, so kind words to a battered soul can bring nourishment. The crescendo to the chapter is the final verse that states, "The lips of the righteous know what finds favor, but the mouth of the wicked only what is perverse" (Proverbs 10:32). There is power in the tongue—for good or for evil. This chapter shows the ability of the tongue to give life, wisdom, and nourishment to many, and at the same time, it reveals the power of the tongue to destroy. So let's consider the impact of our words on others.

- Words can damage your soul as well as others. Our words may not be as dramatic as in the illustration I used earlier, but there are times that they can cause hurt. Proverbs 12:18 says, "The words of the reckless pierce like swords, but the tongue of the wise brings healing." Which tongue do you desire to have? Do you want to be reckless or wise? Do not blame other people for the things you say. Never say, "If you hadn't made me angry, I would not have said that." You are the only person who can guard what comes out of your mouth. Other people can never be blamed for the words that you have spoken. We have to take responsibility for our words as well as our actions. Proverbs 21:23 says, "Those who guard their mouths and their tongues keep themselves from calamity."

Your words can damage others and, in the process, destroy your own spirit. James 3:6 says, "The tongue also is a fire, a world of evil among the parts of the body. It corrupts the whole body, sets the whole course of one's life on fire, and is itself set on fire by hell." That is a sobering verse and shows how our words can damage not only other people but the entire course of our own life.

- Words can restore your soul and heal others. I use the word *heal* intentionally. Our world is full of dysfunctional, hurting people. There are people who have never known the security of family. Some have lived in dysfunctional homes where they have been exposed to cursing, hated, abuse, and negativity. These are broken people who need healing, and as Christ followers, we have the power to see people helped and healed by speaking discerning, wise, and nourishing words. Perhaps you are struggling in a relationship with someone; ensure that your words do not contribute to the problem, but rather let them be filled with wisdom, discernment, and nourishment. The truth is that when our words are kind, affirming, and healing, they keep our own souls vibrant and refreshed.

Your words can destroy or bring healing; you choose.

Reflection

Write down how negative words have impacted your life. Now write down how positive words have affected you. How can you guard your words so they do not cause damage? Who can you intentionally bless today with kind words?

Prayer

Lord, I want my mouth to bless other people and not hurt them. Help me to be deliberate in watching my mouth and the words that come out. I pray that my words will be a fountain of life and nourishment to people today. Help me to be discerning and to know what is fitting and right to say.

Six Strategies for Dealing with Jealousy

 Reading: Psalm 37

I don't know about you, but it is difficult for me to admit that I have had feelings of jealousy about someone. I never enjoy sharing those raw and earthy parts of my nature. And yet, it is true to say that I have envied some people.

The older I get, the more those feelings seem to diminish. Somehow, as the years whittle away, so too does some of my need to compare and compete, which is what nourishes the seeds of jealousy in the soil of my heart. I am aware of how short life is, and I don't want to waste my time or energy on emotions that damage my soul. I know that jealousy is one of those emotions that can inflict harm on me. Although the psalm in our reading uses the word *envious* only once, it reveals the contrast between the person who is wicked and envious and the person who is righteous and kind.

So what are some of the strategies we need to put in place in our lives when we feel those waves of envy rising in our souls and drowning out the passion we have for life and godliness?

- Speak to your soul. The psalmist, speaking to his own soul, asks the question, "Why, my soul, are you downcast? Why so disturbed within me? Put your hope in God, for I will yet praise him, my Savior and my God" (Psalm 42:5). There is something cathartic about speaking to your soul. In this case, the psalmist was despondent, but when you are angry or jealous or any other emotion is seeking to hold you in its grasp, then you need to speak to your own heart and challenge the destructive emotion.

  James 3:16 says, "For where you have envy and selfish ambition, there you find disorder and every evil practice." Jealousy brings the worst out of a person. Bitterness and envy are bedfellows that ignite each other and can light a flame that becomes all consuming. In times when I have felt these emotions rear their ugly heads and realise they are doing me no good, I look at myself in the mirror and speak to myself, reminding myself that I was made in God's image, and when jealousy pervades my spirit, it makes me less human and less like Jesus.

- Be content in your own skin. Remember that you are made in the image of God and His fingerprints are all over you. Psalm 139:14 says, "I praise you because I am fearfully and wonderfully made; your works are wonderful. I know that full well." Let the truth of this text seep into your soul right now. You are created in God's image; He does not see your flaws because He made you, and in His eyes, He made something good. Don't place yourself in juxtaposition with another person because most of the time, it will cause feelings of inferiority or envy. The only one you should strive to imitate is Jesus. Proverbs 14:30 says, "A heart at peace gives life to the body, but envy rots the bones." Have you ever been around tranquil people? It is inspiring to be in their company. They don't have selfish ambitions, they don't have envy, they are content in their skin. They have nothing to prove. You will appear your most beautiful when you are your most tranquil and at peace with yourself and the way God made you.

- Do not feed your jealousy. The seeds of envy can only grow in the soil of your heart when you nurture those cells. Don't dwell on other's blessings or on their abilities and gifts; be grateful for your life. If a particular person is causing you feelings of envy, take some action. If you follow them on social media, quit following them. Don't feed your jealousy by occupying your mind with that person; pour water on those flames so that they die.
- Pray for a spirit of love. Yes, I know it is difficult, but the Bible encourages us to love others. 1 Corinthians 13:4 says, "Love is patient, love is kind. It does not envy, it does not boast, it is not proud." Ask God to replace those feelings of envy with love. I guarantee you that you will feel like a new and healthy person on the inside.
- Make a decision to quit envy today. Make a cold, calculated decision to put jealousy and envy behind you. This loathsome emotion does not produce nice people. There is no miraculous cure for dealing with a negative emotion like this. The only way to move forward is to decide that you are going to deal a death blow to envy. You won't suddenly find those feelings fizzle into thin air; no, it will take daily discipline of your heart and mind to throw water on the flames of jealousy, but eventually, it will be quenched.
- Trust in the Lord. Yes, put your trust in the Lord. I know this might sound trite, but simple trust is precisely what is most needed for the envious heart. Psalm 37:1–4 says, "Do not fret because of those who are evil or be envious of those who do wrong; for like the grass they will soon wither, like green plants they will soon die away. Trust in the Lord and do good; dwell in the land and enjoy safe pasture. Take delight in the Lord, and he will give you the desires of your heart."

Pause now. Ponder what you have just read. When your focus is on the Lord and not on another person, and when your trust is in Him, then He gives you the desires of your heart. Perhaps the person you envy is not an evil person, but like all of us, they will soon fade. Life is short; don't waste your emotions on jealousy. Give them away in generous love. Think of all the wonderful people in your life, and lavish them with love.

My friend, jealousy and envy are harmful emotions. They need to be dealt a death blow. Don't waste your life on destructive emotions when there is so much living to do, so much love to give away, and so much kindness we can do for others.

Reflection

Write down any envious thoughts you have about another person. Pause and read what you have written. Now be intentional in writing about the unique gifts and talents you have. Make a decision today that you will put jealousy in the past. Write down three ways in which you are going to deal with this negative emotion.

Prayer

God, I want my heart to be filled with love and gratitude for all that You have so bountifully lavished on me. Help me to love those who appear to be in a much better place than I am. Help me to dwell on You and Your goodness and help me to put simple trust in You. I pray for Your help in extinguishing jealousy from my heart. May the seeds of love and kindness grow in my soul and help me to express Your love today.

Singing in the Rain

 Readings: Psalm 30; Acts 16:16–40

My life has been a full and adventurous one. I married the man of my dreams. Our marriage has been a wonderful journey of faith, triumph, challenge, and joy. Along the way, I have learned a few things, but one of the most important lessons I learned is to not only sing in the sunshine, but also in the rain. Acts 16:25 says, "About midnight Paul and Silas were praying and singing hymns to God, and the other prisoners were listening to them." Even in prison, in the midst of awful conditions, Paul and Silas chose to sing and praise God. It's easy to sing when things are good, but when things are challenging, it's something we can all do, if we choose.

- Singing in the rain is a discipline. In our reading today, we read a psalm that is filled with praise and thanksgiving, even in the midst of pain. The psalmist says, "Sing the praises of the Lord, you his faithful people; praise his holy name" (Psalm 30:4). Whether it is in the sunshine or the rain, this is a discipline to be nurtured.

 Some people think you have to be born with a certain personality to know the type of joy that causes you to sing in the rain, but the truth is that contentment is a discipline of the heart and mind, and something that all of us can learn. Stop making excuses and blaming your DNA or claiming that your personality is intrinsically melancholic and therefore you are predisposed to being discontented. No, you are a Christ follower; you are transformed into the likeness of Jesus, and that transformation is significantly more powerful than the personality you were born with.

- Singing in the rain is a choice. Perhaps you got up this morning, and from the second the alarm went off, things started to go wrong. You have one of two choices: To sing in the rain or to be deluged by it. I know that some people reading this may be going through challenging experiences; however, you can choose how you will navigate this day. I am certain we all have days when we feel overwhelmed and sad. There is something about singing or listening to a song and singing along that can brighten and even change your day.

  There were times in my life, I felt grief wash over me like a torrent, and I thought I would be entirely swept away. I wasn't. God saw me through. He was there; He held me tight, and when darkness blanketed my soul, threatening to suffocate my faith, somewhere from the black hole, a hand lifted me up, and He put a song in my heart that I could never have sung in my own strength. I have learned to sing both in the sunshine and in the rain.

- Singing in the rain can change circumstances. When you start to sing in the rain, the bread and soup you are eating instead of steak and mushrooms taste wonderful. The old sofa that could not be replaced feels comfortable and comforting. The job you have is not what you wanted, but it is providing for your family; the relationship that went sour is sad, but somehow, Jesus has put new hope in your heart for the next season. Try singing in the rain because it changes everything—the way you feel, the way you perceive, and the way you live.

My prayer is that as you read this devotion, you will make a choice to sing in the sunshine and in the rain. If it is raining today, sing louder; drown out the fear and the sorrow with the sound of your voice. Drown out the shame and the failure with the melody in your heart; whatever you do, keep on singing. Life is too short to miss the opportunity of standing in the pouring rain and singing your heart out. I love what the despondent psalmist said to the Lord: "You turned my wailing into dancing; you removed my sackcloth and clothed me with joy, that my heart may sing your praises and not be silent. Lord my God, I will praise you forever" (Psalm 30:11–12). Make a decision to remove your sackcloth and put on a garment of praise.

Reflection

Write down a song that you can sing in your difficult night. Start singing it now. Make a decision to fill your heart with a melody, and be determined to keep singing in the rain.

Prayer

Lord, I want my heart to be filled with song, even in the midst of my dark night. Help me to sing in the sunshine and in the rain.

The Difference between Being Nice and Being Kind

 Reading: Ephesians 4

Many years ago, our family was enjoying a meal at our dinner table. Our mealtime is never quiet—there is a lot of talking, too much laughing, and way too much eating. For some reason, we got on to a topic that ignited a flame of anger in me about a past hurt. My voice laced with emotion, I expressed myself in no uncertain terms to my family. Words tumbled rapidly off my lips, and there was no doubting that I felt strongly about the issue.

My daughter, usually a person of few words, looked up at me and said, "Mom, you need to build a bridge and get over it."

I was taken aback, to say the least. I knew I had mentioned this issue previously, and I felt that my comments were entirely justified. However, Anna stopped me in my tracks and made me think about what I had said, but more than that, she challenged me to think seriously about my attitude.

My daughter was not nice. But she was kind. In the passage, we read today the apostle Paul exhorts, "Instead speaking the truth in love, we will grow to become in every respect the mature body of him who is the head, that is, Christ" (Ephesians 4:15). Simply put, it is only when we speak the truth, or receive the truth spoken by someone to us (which may not be nice, but is undoubtedly kind), that we can become the fully mature people that Paul exhorts us to be.

You see there is a difference between being nice and being kind. If Anna wanted to be nice to me, she would have sympathized with me and made me feel justified about my poor attitude, or perhaps she could have sat quietly and listened and nodded her head in sympathy and agreement. But then I know that Anna understood that to be silent is to be complicit. If she had simply been nice, she would have pandered to my outburst and allowed me to continue along the pathway to further anger and continued indulgence in my pity party. Instead, she kindly rebuked my attitude so that I could get over the issue.

If I tell my friend who cannot sing in tune that she has a sweet voice, I might be considered nice, but I am certainly not kind. If I tell her she has many great gifts, but singing is not one of them, then she may not consider me the nicest person, but she could never accuse me of not being kind.

Anna is not the only person who has challenged my poor attitudes. There are many other people who have not been nice to me, but in so doing, have been kind. I am thankful to each one of the people who have challenged me in my journey to build and bridge and get over it.

If you have found yourself harping about an issue, replaying hurts over and again in your mind, telling your spouse or family perpetually of your anger about a particular situation, let me take this opportunity to be kind to you and make a few simple suggestions. These few points are probably not going to make you feel all warm and fuzzy inside, but I hope they will challenge you to move forward:

- Acknowledge your problem. No one wants to hear the same old story over and over. This is especially true if the story is not a good one. If your heart is full of anger or hurt, and you find yourself repeating the facts over and over, you have a problem. You need to recognize this so that you can move forward. Yes, I know I am not being nice, but I hope you will see that I am trying to be kind.

- Repent of your attitude. No, don't wait for an apology from the person who has offended you. And no, don't pray that God will judge that person. The person who has hurt or angered you is God's problem. You are the only person who can protect your heart, so ensure that you keep it from anger and bitterness. God wants you to repent of your attitude.

- Move forward. God gave you two eyes, a nose, and a mouth in the front of your face. He gave you two feet that face forward. Everything about His design of our physical being was to move us forward and not backwards. Don't keep looking back and going over old ground. Let go of the issue, and move forward into the future.

- Place measures in your life to ensure you don't go backward. Make yourself accountable to someone; ask them to challenge you if you bring up the old hurt, anger, or bitterness. Ensure that you keep a check on your soul on a daily basis. Read the Bible, speak to God on a regular basis, and find a community that will help you through your times of need. Ephesians 4:29 says, "Do not let any unwholesome talk come out of your mouths, but only what is helpful for building others up according to their needs, that it may benefit those who listen." This verse explains the essence of what being kind is all about. Being nice is not wholesome for us or for anyone else; being kind is building other people up according to their need.

The great news, my friend, is that no experience is ever wasted. Even our hurtful experiences are not pointless. If we keep our hearts right, God will take our past experiences and channel them to make us better, stronger, and more effective for His kingdom. So, my friend, in the words of my daughter, build a bridge and get over it. Why let the hurts, failures, anger, or bitterness of yesterday limit your today? Move forward into the incredible, bright future God has for you.

The chapter we read ends with a wonderful exhortation for us to take into our day: "Be kind and compassionate to one another, forgiving each other, just as Christ in God forgave you."

Reflection

Is there someone in your life you need to show kindness to? Write down how you are going to achieve this goal. Is there an anger issue in your life that needs dealing with? Reflect on it, write it down, and then decide how you will move forward, and let the past be left behind.

Prayer

God, help me to be deliberate in moving forward. Thank You for the people in my life who have been kind enough to show me where I fall short. Help me in my shortcomings so that I can grow in You. Help me to be kind and honest with those who need my kindness today.

Think before You Gossip

 Readings: James 1:26; 2 Corinthians 12:20; Proverbs 10:18, 11:12–13, 16:28

You start out conversing with someone, and before you know it, the conversation has taken you down the slippery slope of gossip. It can begin quite innocently. You start out with friendly chatter, and then someone asks a question about another person, and before you know it, the conversation is full of juicy morsels of unkind words and gossip. Truth be told, we have probably all been guilty of going down that road and sometimes enjoying it more than we should have. But, generally speaking, the aftertaste in your mouth is unpleasant because you said things that should never have been voiced.

Our readings today are different from other devotions. We look at a couple of New Testament passages as well as a number of verses from Proverbs. Each text speaks specifically to the issue at hand and warns us against gossip.

Before you gossip next time, please consider the following questions:

- Are you talking to the right person? If you need to speak to someone about a particular issue, then make sure you are speaking to the right person. Generally, when you are speaking to someone else about another person, it is or tends to lead to gossip. Not always, but most times.

- Are you enjoying the conversation? Is it making you feel good to vent about this particular person? Are you feeling satisfied about what you are saying? When you are unkind about a person and feel good about venting and being critical, it is just plain gossip. Alternatively, when you leave a conversation and feel a tinge of regret and remorse for what you have said, this too is a sure sign that you were involved in gossip.

- Are you couching your gossip behind spiritual language? Oftentimes, the conversation begins with a spiritual tone that can go something like this: "I am looking for some advice about ..." Or worse still, "Can we pray about ... I am concerned about their well-being because ..." or "Can you give me some wisdom when I deal with ... her life is in a mess." If we are concerned about a person, then we should be addressing them, not talking about them to someone else.

- Are you full of rancor? If you are, then you are gossiping. Saying something unkind about people when they are not present is without a doubt gossip. That lacks compassion and is divisive.

- Would Jesus approve of what you are saying? That is a fairly simple question, right? Then next time you are tempted to say something unkind about someone, ask yourself this question.

- When was the last time you prayed for this person? Imagine if all the time you spend in slander you spent in prayer for this person. It would make a difference in them and in you.

- Will the person you are talking to be able to help the situation? Another easy question, right? If they cannot help the person you are talking about, then why are you even talking to them?

- Will the person you are talking about be helped by your conversation? If the answer is a resounding no, then it is gossip.

The world would be a much happier place without gossip-mongers. Let me assure you that no gossip has ever produced any good. Honest conversations and speaking the truth in love to the person will achieve far more than gossip ever will.

So next time you are in the company of gossipers, stop the conversation or challenge the gossiper. Gossip destroys lives, sows conflict, raises doubts, causes suspicion, alienates friends, and shatters communities. Who wants to be guilty of any of those consequences? What you say is more impactful than you think. Make sure your words are wise, kind, and fitting. Give someone the gift of kind and generous words today. It will make their day better and yours too.

 Reflection

Write down the names of people who you know have gossiped about you and hurt you. Stop now and pray for them. Now write down the names of people that you have gossiped about. Pray for them. What measures will you take to avoid gossip?

 Prayer

God, enable me to use my words wisely. Help me to avoid idle chatter that leads to gossip. Help my spoken words to honor You throughout this day. I pray for those who have hurt me with their unkind gossip. I ask You to forgive me for the unkind words I have freely spoken about some of Your children. Help me to express Your love to everyone I come into contact with today.

CAROL ANNE ALEXANDER

Practicing the Fruit
of Self-Control

 Readings: Galatians 5; Romans 8

Many years ago, I knew a lady who constantly made excuses for herself and her husband. They were both professional people, but they had a number of personal issues. She would often say, "People need to learn to accept us as we are, warts and all." The problem was that they had no intention of working on their weaknesses or practicing any kind of self-control or discipline. You can understand why people found them an exasperating couple, and many of their friendships fractured.

Self-control is one of the varieties of the fruit of the Spirit, and one that we all need to practice. The Bible does not imply that this fruit of the Spirit is simply an optional extra. Rather, if we are committed Christ followers, then it is assumed that we will practice the fruit of self-control. That means we are not always making excuses for our flaws, but we are constantly disciplining our lives and stewarding them towards the purposes of God.

So how do we practice the fruit of self-control that Paul speaks about in Galatians 5:22–23?

- Self-control is not a short-term solution. We all have cravings and desires, and it's easy to give in to them. However, Paul says that we have to control those desires, or they will eventually control us. I suppose you could say it is similar to self-discipline. Just as some people are disciplined when it comes to eating and exercise, so too, we should be disciplined when it comes to self. Any craving, desire, or lust that is not wholesome must be controlled. We cannot make excuses. Yes, we are all human, but every one of us has the power to make choices. Your choice can be a good one or a bad one, and that decision is entirely yours. I can guarantee you that there will be consequences for every decision you make—good or bad.

- Self-control builds your character. What does it mean to be a person of character? I would posit that it is being consistent and doing what is right, even when no one is looking. Character is doing what is good and honorable, even when the wrong thing is legal or acceptable to other people. Good character is sorely lacking in our world. When we hear vitriolic hatred, racial slurs, or demeaning comments spewing from a person, we immediately know that their character is lacking because there is no evidence of self-control.

Some people have weaknesses in their lives that are different from those that others face. But truth be told, we all have weaknesses that we need to address. We must ensure that we are constantly working on those areas of our lives that seek to bring us into bondage. You don't practice self-control for a day and then give up. No. This is a lifelong discipline, but like any exercise, it becomes easier with time. Take courage in your journey. We read in Romans 8:26, "In the same way, the Spirit helps us in our weakness." The truth is that we do not struggle on our own; we have the help of God's Spirit, and He enables us even in our weakness.

- Self-control is dying to self. There is a battle that goes on inside of us. Paul spoke about that struggle in Romans. Our carnal side (the human, fleshly part of our humanity) is battling against our spiritual side. We need to die to the carnal or fleshly part of our nature so that our spiritual one will grow. The more you feed that carnal aspect of your life, the weaker the spiritual part of you is, and vice versa. So feed and nourish the spiritual part of your humanity. The apostle Paul put it clearly when he said in Romans 8:13–14, "For if you live according to the flesh, you will die; but if by the Spirit you put to death the misdeeds of the body, you will live. For those who are led by the Spirit of God are the children of God."

Self-control is a discipline that we all need to practice on a daily basis. Don't make excuses; surrender yourself to a loving God, and ask Him for His help today. He wants you to live your life successfully and well, and to do so requires the fruit of self-control.

Reflection

Write down the areas of your life where you lack self-control. Be honest. Now write down what you will do to feed the spiritual side of your life so that you can starve the carnal part. Read Galatians 5 slowly and prayerfully one more time.

Prayer

God, I acknowledge my weaknesses to You. I pray for Your help as I navigate the challenges of life today. Help me to exhibit self-control in every area of my life. I want to be consistent in my life. I need Your help to feed the spiritual part of my being so that I can starve the carnal side. Help me to develop this fruit consistently and on a daily basis, I pray.

Winning the Battle

 Reading: 2 Corinthians 10

Life is filled with challenges. Navigating difficulties with grace is important for our souls. As I reflect over the years, there have been times I did not navigate some of those challenges well, and there are a number of lessons I learned along the way that I now share with you. When there is a battle of any kind, there are two opposing opinions or more. The battle is because two people see things differently. These battles can become all-consuming and get completely out of control. As I have contemplated the battles I have faced, here are some principles I have learned:

- Conquer pride with humility. Whenever we face a battle or a challenge, our pride tends to push its way to the surface. The most natural human tendency is to defend ourselves and our reputation. I have discovered that God does a much better job of protecting our reputation than we do. When we yield to pride and break other people down to defend ourselves, it may have an immediate impact by making other people look bad, but what does that do in the long term? The better way by far is to take the advice of Paul found in Philippians 2:6–7, where he says of Jesus, "Who, being in very nature God, did not consider equality with God something to be used to his own advantage; rather, he made himself nothing by taking the very nature of a servant, being made in human likeness." Jesus modelled a better way for us and showed us what humility really looked like. So if you are in a battle, don't lash out with pride and criticism; take the higher ground, and be humble and allow God to intervene in the situation.

- Conquer division with unity. We cannot agree with other people all the time. However, there is a way to disagree agreeably. Of course, we can disagree; sometimes, we should. It is important to be able to express our opinions with grace and in a way that does not cause division. We see acrimony and division in the political world, and most of us are repulsed by it. I do believe that it is vital that as Christians, we express our convictions with civility. When we express our convictions with the purpose of dividing and harming, then we can cause irreparable harm, and it does nothing to solve the problem or bring lasting resolve. The only way to navigate division is to have your eye on unity.

- Conquer war with peace. As a Christian leader, I have often walked into war zones. No, not literal war zones, but situations where there was anger and strife. When we invite Jesus to come in, and there is repentance, forgiveness, humility, and grace, it is amazing how peace can permeate the situation and bring change. This is the way of Jesus. I do believe that sowing peace in perilous situations is the only way to bring resolve.

- Conquer foolishness with wisdom. There can be occasions when we think our way is best, but sometimes, it is not. If there is anger, resentment, or bitterness in your heart, you are on thin ice. In times of anger, we can say foolish things and respond in silly ways. My humble advice is to pause and allow God to give you wisdom for the situation you are navigating. Deal with the root of anger so you don't say foolish things that bring no resolve. Don't open your mouth while there is anger in your heart because you will probably say the wrong thing. Ask God for His wisdom for the situation you are facing.

It is important to remember that our battle is in the unseen world. 2 Corinthians 10 makes it clear that the weapons we use are not the same ones the world uses. We should never lash out with unkind words. We should resist criticism and avoid being mean-spirited because our battle is ultimately not with people; rather, it is a battle taking place in the unseen world. The most powerful weapons we have against spiritual forces are prayer and simple trust. Let us not resort to the weapons of this world but use the resources that God put at our disposal. And those resources are plentiful. The Lord promises us wisdom and help for these situations, so we should avail ourselves of them.

Reflection

Write about the battle you are facing or one you are helping other people to navigate. Pause now, and ask God for wisdom in this problem. What can you do to bring an end to this division? Write down three ways in which you seek to resolve the situation you are dealing with.

🙏 Prayer

God, I am in the midst of a battle. I am asking You for wisdom in negotiating this issue. I pray for a spirit of humility that enables me to do what is right and to say what will bring healing in the midst of hurt. I want to see unity and not division; help me to do my part in accomplishing this.

Facts Are Your Friends,
Not Your Foes

 Reading: Psalm 55

Sometimes, it is easier or more comfortable to deny our current reality than to face up to it. We see the brutal facts and don't like them, and so we try to hide from them, run from them, deny them, or pray against them. I have been in that situation before. I detested what I was facing, and so in order to navigate around the problem, I either denied it flat out or prayed fervently against my reality. The truth is, none of that helped me, and it did not help the situation I was facing. You see, facts are our friends, not our enemies.

This week might find you facing some difficulty or challenge in your life, your ministry, your workplace, or your relationships. You may be finding it challenging to navigate the situation you are currently facing. Here are a few suggestions that I believe could help you through your difficulties:

- Face the facts. If you have been told that you have a terminal disease, then the best thing you can do is to face your reality. You can confront it with strength and courage, or you can choose to deny it. If you look at the facts and accept them as your reality, it will help you to make wise decisions in moving forward. The same goes for a relationship that has failed or a job that has ended or any other situation you might be facing. Consider the facts, be honest about them, and then make a decision on how you will move forward and navigate your current reality. Denying the facts will not help you, your situation, or anyone else; it will only lengthen the process and the agony. Denial will only make your journey more arduous.

I had a friend who had a very sick family member. She kept pronouncing that he wasn't ill. She thought that denying illness meant that she had a strong faith. In fact, the only consequence of her denial was that it kept her from making wise decisions about his medical treatment, which he desperately needed. Facing facts is not easy, but it is best.

- Facts and faith work together. When you have all the facts, and you face your current reality and then marry it with faith, you have the ingredients for a miracle. The Bible teaches us to look to Jesus in the midst of our reality and challenge. Hebrews 12:1–2 says, "Therefore, since we are surrounded by such a great cloud of witnesses, let us throw off everything that hinders and the sin that so easily entangles. And let us run with perseverance the race marked out for us, fixing our eyes on Jesus, the pioneer and perfecter of faith. For the joy set before him he endured the cross, scorning its shame, and sat down at the right hand of the throne of God."

After Jay had his car accident, the doctors told us that he would not survive, and we had to face our reality square on. There was no denying it because he was on life support for twenty-eight days. We knew he was hovering between life and death; he was in a critical situation. These dreadful facts did not negate my faith; they strengthened it. I knew that medical science, with all the incredible progress it had made, had its limitations, but I knew that with my God, the impossible becomes possible. My faith was strengthened by the gruesome facts. I did not like them; my pain was intense, but the brutal facts certainly made my faith strong. Facing the facts also helped us to make the kind of medical decisions that would benefit Jay.

- Facts are not the enemy. Facts will not destroy you as a person; it is how you respond to the facts that is vital to your well-being. If you are facing financial challenges, do not deny your reality; face it, pray about it, ask God to help you, make good decisions, cut your cloth according to size, and navigate your reality with the Lord at your side. If you are struggling with a broken relationship, admit the brutal facts, do your best to mend the fractures, and put your simple trust in God to work with you through the challenge. The same applies to any and every situation that you are confronting; face the facts, do what you can, and pray earnestly for God's help.

My friend, we all go through challenging and stretching times. Facing your current reality with courage and simple trust in God is the only reasonable pathway to take. Don't try to manage this situation on your own; give your reality to God, look it square in the eye, pray for wisdom, and ask Him to help you navigate this journey with grace and courage.

I leave you with a verse from Isaiah 41:13: "For I am the Lord your God who takes hold of your right hand and says to you, Do not fear; I will help you." This was an ancient promise that God gave to His people, but His promises still stand today. He will be with you through your difficult season; allow Him to hold your hand through the struggles of life. Put your hand in His today, and let Him guide you through your reality; don't do it on your own. He wants to walk with you through your challenges and trials.

In our reading today, the psalmist is crying out to God about his troubles. His heart is in anguish, and he is ready to run from his reality. At a certain point in agony, he cries out boldly, "Cast your cares on the Lord and He will sustain you; he will never let the righteous be shaken" (Psalm 55:22). Friend, no matter how difficult your current reality might be, God is with you. He invites you to throw your worries and anxieties on Him. Your reality may seem untenable at this time, but remember, God will uphold you. Trust Him. The final phrase echoed from the psalmist's lips is heartfelt: "But as for me, I trust in you" (Psalm 55:23). Simple trust will enable you to face the facts and navigate the challenges with God at your side.

 Reflection

Write down what your current reality is. What are you going to do to face this reality? What are you asking God to do in the midst of this challenge? Think of two tangible things you can do to confront your reality. Write them down, and ask God to help you in your commitment.

 Prayer

God, I need Your help to see me through this challenging time of life. Help me to face the facts and marry them with the simple faith I have learned about in this devotional. I know that You are teaching me to put my trust in You as I navigate my reality. Hold me fast, and help me to achieve my goal.

Four Reasons Why
You Should Pray

 Readings: Luke 18; Matthew 6:1–14

My husband, Paul, and I start every morning with prayer. Many times, we spontaneously begin our prayer time with thanksgiving and praise. As I reflect over the past number of years, I have seen God answer my prayers over and again.

I love our times of speaking to our heavenly Father, and I can honestly say they are some of the most valuable moments in my day. I do not know how I would sustain my life without the discipline of prayer. Colossians 4:2 says, "Devote yourselves to prayer, being watchful and thankful." We are exhorted to be committed to prayer and in so doing to be cautious in living as well as thankful for everything.

Here are four reasons why you should pray.

- You can trust your heavenly Father. It never ceases to amaze me that this wonderful God Who created the heavens and the earth is a personal God and wants a relationship with His children. Psalm 9:10 says, "Those who know your name trust in you, for you, Lord, have never forsaken those who seek you." I am daily overawed by the fact that I can go boldly into God's presence and talk to Him. Those moments of intimacy with Him are precious and life-giving, and He hears what we cannot even put in words; He reads our hearts. Psalm 34:15 says, "The eyes of the Lord are on the righteous, and his ears are attentive to their cry." I have come to depend upon my moments with God, and I know beyond a shadow of a doubt that the rhythm of my life is dependent upon these moments of intimacy.

- You can be vulnerable with your heavenly Father. We never have to pretend with God. He knows our hearts even better than we know ourselves. Psalm 38:9 says, "All my longings lie open before you, Lord: my sighing is not hidden from you." God knows us so intimately that He even hears our sighs. When you go to Him in prayer, you can praise. You can vent. You can repent. You can request. The truth is, you can open your heart to your God and be honest with Him. Share with your Father your dreams, heartaches, desires, visions, and hopes; spill your heart out to Him. I sometimes wonder if my dreams are too big, and then I am reminded that God is the giver of dreams. There is no dream too big or too small for Him. People may chuckle at your dreams, but God won't. He never dampens any dream. He puts His arms around us and tells us to keep dreaming and trusting in Him because He knows best. Simple trust is what we need. The prayer in our reading today guides us to ask our Father for what we need, for forgiveness of sins, and for deliverance from temptation.

- You can find strength for the day from your heavenly Father. What a thought. Hebrews 4:16 says, "Let us then approach God's throne of grace with confidence, so that we may receive mercy and find grace to help us in our time of need." When you feel weak, inadequate, incapable, exhausted, or broken, you can find strength as you put your simple trust in God. This is not a time to withdraw from God but a time to find the help and strength you need.

- You need to be persistent in prayer. Sometimes, we get lackadaisical in our prayer life. We may have been praying about something for so long that we become weary. However, the Bible encourages us to be persistent in our prayers. In an earlier devotion we read in 1 Kings 18 how Elijah prayed until the rain came. He did not give up praying, and as you read in this next verse, he persisted for seven times until he knew God had answered him: "The seventh time the servant reported, 'A cloud as small as a man's hand rising from the sea'" (1 Kings 18:44).

Our reading in Luke tells the story of the widow who kept persisting with her request before the judge. He refused her over and over, but eventually, he gave in to the widow's persistent plea. Jesus exhorts us to the same persistence in our prayer life. You may be tired of laying your request before God, but keep praying and persisting, because He is working on your behalf, even if you cannot see it. Further on in the passage in Luke, Jesus heals the blind beggar, who kept shouting out, "Son of David, have mercy on me" (Luke 18:39). He was rebuked by many in the crowd, but that did not stop him from shouting even louder. Jesus did not turn a deaf ear to his cry but stopped and asked the man what he wanted.

"'Lord, I want to see,' he replied" (Luke 18:41). Jesus knew the heart of people, and I am persuaded He knew what the blind man needed, but Jesus wanted to hear the man articulate his desire. What do we read next? "Immediately he received his sight and followed Jesus, praising God. When all the people saw it, they also praised God" (Luke 18:43). The blind man would not be put off by the rebukes of people, the noise, the mob, the excitement; nothing hindered him from shouting out his request to the Lord. Keep shouting, keep asking, be persistent because God is listening.

I have found prayer to be one of the most important aspects in the rhythm of my day. Over the years, I have learned the value of prayer. The more I talk to my heavenly Father, the more my trust grows. I used to talk to people about my problems and wondered why they were never resolved. When I started taking my needs and anxieties to God, I found not only peace for my soul, but grace to sustain me through my distress. Take some time to pause today and take your needs to the Lord.

Reflection

Write down your prayer to God today. Open your heart to Him, and remember He understands you and knows you intimately. You can be totally vulnerable with God. Express your heart's desire to Him on this page.

Prayer

God, I am so thankful that I come bring my requests to You. Not only can I lay them before You, but I can bring them boldly into Your presence. Thank You that You know my heart. I do not have to hide anything from You. Please see my heart today and hear the words that are deep within my heart but I cannot articulate.

Does God Always Answer Our Prayers?

 Reading: Psalm 34

God, are you listening to me? Why aren't you answering my prayers? Do you love me? Are you mad at me? Valid questions, right? Yes, and I am sure most of us have asked these questions at different times in our lives. But when we understand God in all His omnipotence, then we can stop questioning Him, rest in who He is, and wait for Him to answer in His way. That requires simple trust.

Crying, pleading, and at times begging God to answer my prayers had been the content of much of my prayer life. "Where are You, God?" I would often ask. Silence and darkness were at times the only reply. I simply did not understand why my loving God was not hearing me, or so I thought.

Truth be told, He was listening. His loving and attentive ear was hearing my cry, even though I felt that He wasn't. I have learned that faith should not be held captive by my feelings.

- Feeling bad doesn't mean God has abandoned you. He is bigger than our feelings or emotions on any particular day.

Malachi 3:6 says, "I the Lord do not change." Thankfully, the Lord does not have mood swings, and He does keep His promises. My feelings do not change God. He hears my cry, when I am feeling good or bad. God is a consistent God, who loves His children with an everlasting love. His ear is always open to our cry. Our reading today says, "The eyes of the Lord are on the righteous, and his ears are attentive to their cry" (Psalm 34:15). Our emotions shift, but the Lord never changes, and His ears are always open to our plea.

- God answers prayers on His clock and not on ours. We live in time, but God lives in eternity. Understand that we are eternal beings living in the temporal, bound by time and space. We get caught up in the day-to-day activity of our lives and don't see the end from the beginning, as God does. This verse has always encouraged my heart: "All the days ordained for me were written in your book before one of them came to be" (Psalm 139:16). God does see the big picture because He is eternal. He knows best and will answer in His time, and His timing is always perfect. It is our responsibility to seek the Lord and then wait patiently for His answer.

- God doesn't always answer our prayers in the way we anticipate. At times, I give God some great suggestions as to how He can answer my prayers. I lay a carefully crafted plan before Him and tell Him how He can get it fulfilled. He seldom if ever adheres to my clever ideas. That is because God is infinitely cleverer than I am. I have to remind myself that God sees the end from the beginning, and He knows how best and when best to answer my prayers.

- God sees what we do not see. There have been times I have felt that my request to Him fell on deaf ears. I have felt discouraged and lost heart. Years passed, and I have seen how wise God was in not answering my prayer in the way I wanted Him to. He saw things that I could not possibly know or anticipate, and I'm so thankful for Him wisely withholding my request. I did not understand it then, but I do now.

My friend, if you are struggling with your prayer life, then I trust that this devotional encourages you. Don't give up. God's answer will come in His way and His time. I am filled with thanksgiving as I reflect on the faithful and loving God I serve. He always answers prayer, even when it is not obvious to me.

The Bible gives us some sound advice when it says, "Wait for the Lord; be strong and take heart and wait for the Lord" (Psalm 27:14). Keep praying; keep trusting. His answer will come.

Reflection

Get your pen and tell God exactly how you feel in this moment. Be vulnerable because He understands. Now write down your requests on this page. Look over what you have read and then pray the prayer below.

Prayer

God, I sometimes feel as if You are far away. I acknowledge that it is simply my own perspective, and my trust is not dependent upon my feelings. Help me to focus on You throughout this day. I want to learn to trust You more. Make me more aware of Your presence, and help me to grow in my prayer life so I can draw closer to You day by day. Help me to learn that simple trust in You enables me to leave everything in Your hands, to trust in Your perfect timing, and to grasp that You have my best interests at heart.

How to Prevent Burnout

 Reading: Psalm 23

It seems that people living in the twenty-first century suffer from burnout more than in previous eras. Burnout is stress and sheer exhaustion mixed with a sense of disillusionment, helplessness, and hopelessness. The problem with this malady is that it can threaten many aspects of your life. It can damage your own personal health and well-being; it can negatively impact your relationships, and it can be hazardous for your career. Burnout can be a serious and debilitating state; we shouldn't minimize it, but do everything we can to prevent it.

So how do we prevent burnout?

I have a few simple guidelines to put in place in our lives to ensure that we never allow ourselves to get into this situation:

- Don't ignore fatigue. There have been times when I have pushed myself beyond my limits; I have worked until midnight and then started working again at 5 a.m. I did not experience burnout, but my body did tell me that it resented what I was doing to it, and the result was four weeks of vertigo. If I had kept going at that pace, I would have exhausted myself physically, mentally, emotionally, and spiritually. The result of all of that pushing would probably have been burnout.

We need to listen to our bodies and not ignore them or simply push through our fatigue. Of course, there are times when I am tired and need to keep working; however, that is different from pushing myself beyond reasonable limits. I have to remind myself that when my soul is shattered and weary, the Shepherd is there to refresh me if I avail myself of His promise. And if the Lord is my Shepherd, then I am safe in His care as long as I stay close to Him.

- Recognize your limitations. You have to come to terms with your humanity and your own limitations. Some people have a capacity for work that others may not have. Over the years, Paul and I have developed an internal resilience for the kind of work we do. Not everybody could keep our pace. There are people who do manual work that I would never have the resilience for. We have to be conscious of our capacity and know our limitations and listen to our bodies. Blaise Pascal said it this way: "We must learn our limits. We are all something, but none of us are everything." Admitting you are human with limitations will help you to channel the gifts and abilities you have in the right direction and will help to maximize God's plans for you.

- Learn to say no. I am certainly not encouraging laziness. A good day's work never killed anyone. Laziness is not a characteristic to be admired. However, there are times in our lives where we have to say no to certain things. You are the only person who can do this; you have to be discerning of what to agree to. That is your call. Don't try to be a people-pleaser; rather, be honest about your capacity and be ready to say no if you have to.

- You are not indispensable. Sometimes, we think we are the only one in the world who can do the task properly. Realize that you are not irreplaceable. The world will still keep turning when you are gone. It is good to recognize you are not superhuman.
- Balance every part of your life. First, take care of your physical health. Watch what you eat and drink, and ensure that you get exercise. Simply put, be wise with your body. Second, you need to care about your emotional well-being. Ensure that you get some downtime. We all need play time and sleep time as much as we do work time. You will keep your emotional health when you balance all aspects of your life. Third, take good care of your spiritual life. Ensure that you spend time with God, read His Word, and get connected to a church community. Your spiritual well-being is also an important aspect in the prevention of burnout. That is why Psalm 23 is an important text for us. If the Lord is our Shepherd, then this verse we read next becomes meaningful: "He makes me lie down in green pastures, and leads me beside quiet waters, he refreshes my soul" (Psalm 23:2–3).

  If God is the leader of our lives, then "even though I walk through the darkest valley, I will fear no evil, for you are with me; your rod and your staff, they comfort me" (Psalm 23:4). There are great promises in Psalm 23 if we lay hold of them. A promise to refresh you, to sustain you, to comfort you, to lead you, and to guide you, and ultimately for you to dwell with Him forever.

If you are tired and discouraged, and you know that it is more than ordinary stress and tension, then this devotion is for you. You are too important to your family, to God, and to your community to have burnout. Read Psalm 23 again, and ponder the words carefully. God is your Shepherd, and He wants to lead you beside quiet waters to restore your soul. People need you, depend upon you, and love you. If you attend to your own emotional and spiritual well-being, you will be able to make a more positive contribution to the lives of others. Ensure that you take time to refresh your soul. Prevent burnout or further exhaustion before it is too late.

Reflection

What tasks can you put aside in order to diminish stress in your life? Think carefully about this question. Are you a perfectionist? What tasks can you let go to give yourself time to breathe? Do you need to say no to a project so that you can prioritize your time in a more beneficial way? Be deliberate about reflecting today. Is there someone to who you can make yourself accountable so as to ensure that you stay on track with your goals? Write down at least one task you can step back from, and then pen how you aim to achieve this goal.

Prayer

God, I thank You that You are my Shepherd. I ask You to help me to allow You to lead me to those quiet waters so that I can refresh my soul. I am tired and need Your strength for today. Help me to say no to the things that are unimportant and enable me to prioritize wisely. I want to pause in Your presence for a while and feel Your grace, peace, and strength flow into me. Let Your goodness and love follow me today and all the days of my life.

Run, Baby, Run

 Reading: Genesis 39

Many years ago, when Paul and I were training missionaries in South Africa, we received a phone call from a man in England. He invited us to interview to be the pastors of a thriving church in a beautiful British town. We flew over for the interview, not really knowing what to anticipate.

Three of the leading elders of the church welcomed us and interviewed us for some time. After we finished the interview, they spoke while we sat quietly and listened. We were amazed at what we were being offered: a golden platter filled with many enticing things, including financial resources. And it was tempting, to say the least.

We were going through a difficult patch in our ministry, and this seemingly wonderful opportunity looked like the perfect escape. But not everything that looks good is right for you. And more importantly, it is not necessarily the pathway God wants for your life.

Leaving the interview, we assured the elders that we would prayerfully consider their offer. We prayed about the invitation we had received and felt the Lord did not want us to leave our current ministry. Their offer looked so appealing, especially in light of the many challenges we were facing in our work at that time. I am thankful that we listened to God and went back to our ministry to finish what He had called us to do. I reflect with gratitude over that experience and thank God that He gave us the courage to run from temptation. Yes, I use the word "run" deliberately because even though the offer made to us was a worthy calling, it certainly was not what God wanted for our lives at that time.

Temptation comes in different guises. Let me assure you that the enemy knows your weak spots, and he will attempt to strike there.

- You have to know when to run. Not all temptations are sinister or sexual; some can be subtle and even appear harmless, but when you have discerned the temptation, you need to run. Our invitation, by these elders, to lead a significant church appeared plausible. The church was healthy, the congregation were wonderful, and the elders inviting us were godly men who were looking for a pastor to lead their church. As we prayed, we realized that this was a tempting offer that we had to run from. We had not finished the work God had called us to, and I am quite certain that ministry would not be here today if we had yielded to the offer.
- You have to run immediately. There are some temptations that are far more sinister that we need to flee from. When Potiphar's wife told Joseph she wanted to sleep with him, he ran for his life. He did not wait to contemplate her request. Most temptations do not need any consideration; just put on your running shoes and get out of there as quickly as you can. If you are married, and there is someone you are feeling attracted to—run. Don't throw away everything you have for a few moments of pleasure. Proverbs is right when it says that in the end, it will be

gall in your mouth. When it comes to pornography, put all kinds of safeguards in place. Have a trusted mentor who will hold you accountable. Never go to sites that will harm your soul. True, maybe no one will find out, but your soul will atrophy, and what goes on in the silence of your head will impact every part of your life and your relationships. And even more importantly, God sees everything, and sin hinders our relationship with Him. So run from sin.

- You have to plan your escape route. This route should be planned in advance. In the cold light of day, with your heart open to the Lord, make some choices. This is planning your escape in a careful and considered fashion. Determine that you will honor God all your days. Study the Bible, and memorize portions of it so that you can call them to mind when you need to. If you are committed to God, you will ensure that when temptation comes—as it surely will—you will run from it. Be deliberate and committed in all your relationships, and cherish them. The Bible is wise when it calls us to be faithful to our spouse. Commitment to your marriage will establish a firm and secure future for your family. The greatest gift you can give to your children is your love and devotion to each other. If you make these decisions in the clear light of day, in other words, you have a planned escape route in place, then when temptation comes your way, you know exactly what you have to do.

Finally, be committed to caring for your soul. No one can take responsibility for your soul; only you can. Make your soul accountable to God, but ensure you have a mentor, someone who is willing to ask you the difficult questions. Do anything and everything you can to ensure the health of your soul.

My prayer is that God will protect you and keep you. However, my greater prayer is that you will take responsibility to ensure that you run when temptation comes. Put all the necessary safeguards in place in your life so that when temptation comes your way, you can flee. May your day be blessed and filled with His grace.

Reflection

What safeguards can you put in place in your life to ensure that when temptation comes your way, you do not give in to it? If you are struggling with an issue, tell God about it. Be honest. Have you got a trusted friend or mentor you can talk to, who will hold you accountable? Pause and ask God to lead you to the right person. Now pray the prayer below.

Prayer

God, as I face this day, I ask You for the grace and help I need to live wisely. I want to keep my heart pure and live right. My desire is to honor You in all that I do. I pray that You will help me to flee temptation when it comes my way. Help me to be deliberate and make good choices that lead me to paths of righteousness.

Give Someone a Golden Apple Today

 Reading: Psalm 19

I have already mentioned a number of times how impactful words can be. Have you ever received a kind word or a compliment when you are having a rough day? It is heartwarming, isn't it? Even if your day is going well, generous words can make you glow on the inside. I am sure you also know the opposite is true. When people lash out at you, when angry words fall from their lips, we know the battering our soul takes. That is why James chapter 3 is an important passage to take note of. It warns us about a tongue that is out of control. Proverbs 25:11 says, "Like apples of gold in settings of silver is a ruling rightly given." What a beautiful metaphor showing the impact of wise words, as opposed to a tongue that is unruly.

I never tire of affirmation. My husband can tell me ten times a day that he loves me and appreciates me, but I never grow weary of hearing those words. Why? Because affirming and kind words are like food for our soul.

- Words can harm for a long time. When I was a little girl and nasty friends would say something unkind to me, I would retort, "Sticks and stones can break my bones, but words can never harm me." I realise now that there is no truth to that pithy little rhyme. There are times I would have preferred a physical whipping rather than the lashing my soul received from brutal and unkind words. I also know that when someone has sincerely affirmed me, it has felt like a balm to my soul. The tongue has so much power; words can wound people beyond recovery, or they can heal a broken heart.

- Words can direct or destroy. Your tongue can control the direction of your life and of others. We shape our words, but our words also shape us. Your tongue can control the direction of your life. If you are always negative about yourself, you are shaping your destiny by the shape of your words. Your words can also have a powerful effect on other people. I know when people believed in me and affirmed me, their words helped me take positive steps into my future. There are some things I would never have attempted unless some person had believed in me and encouraged me.

- Silent words are as powerful as spoken ones. The psalmist called our silent words the thoughts of our hearts. "May these words of my mouth and this meditation of my heart be pleasing in your sight, Lord, my Rock and my Redeemer" (Psalm 19:14). No one can hear those words; only you and the Lord know about the words that run through your brain. Those words are as powerful as your spoken words. Don't minimize the effect of your thought life. What you think can make your soul healthy or unwell. If you are always thinking negatively, it will impact every part of your life.

Medical science reveals how the mind and the body work together. When we are negative, it releases all types of harmful chemicals into our bodies. And the same is true when we are positive; we release endorphins into our bloodstream that give us a sense of well-being. Never undermine the impact of those unspoken words that float around your brain. That is why it is so important to discipline our thought life and why the apostle Paul said in Philippians 4:8, "Finally, brothers and sisters, whatever is true, whatever is noble, whatever is right, whatever is pure, whatever is lovely, whatever is admirable—if anything is excellent or praiseworthy—think about such things." Watch your thought life today because the words flowing through your mind are impacting you, either positively or negatively.

Why not use this day to affirm the people around you? When was the last time you really appreciated a family member? Did you affirm them with kind words? Maybe write a letter to someone and give away some gracious words. Be generous with your words. Don't wait for a compliment or look for kind affirmation; be a giver. Lavish kindness on the people around you, and give them a beautiful golden apple today. I can assure you of one thing; no, maybe two: it will change their day, but it will also brighten yours.

Reflection

Be intentional about giving golden apples to people today. Who can you bless with kind and affirming words? How can you watch your silent words to ensure that they are doing you good? Write down ways in which you are going to be deliberate in using your spoken and silent words today.

Prayer

God, thank You that You have spoken good over my life. You have a plan and a future for me that is blessed and good. I pray today that You will help me to put a guard on my mouth. I want my words to bless people today. Help me to give away some golden apples today. Enable me to be generous and sincere with my words. I pray that my silent and my spoken words will honor You throughout this day.

Dealing with Crippling Fear

 Readings: Joshua 1; Nehemiah 2

I have known and experienced fear at different times in my life. When the doctors discovered that Paul had an aortic aneurism and required surgery, I could almost taste the fear. At times, fear would latch onto me and cling to me like a heavy cloud—cold, dark, gray, diffusing into every cell in my body. It would creep up my thighs, enter my belly, and fill my mouth with its metallic taste. I have experienced this emotion in different situations of life, and it can be debilitating. I can only describe it as being in a vortex.

I learned about this invasive emotion we call fear in my psychology class many years before. Fear has its origin in the brain. When people see or hear danger approaching, their senses send this information to a small almond-shaped structure in the brain called the amygdala. This tiny part of the brain transmits the information to the hypothalamus (much like a control center), which then alerts the body via the nervous system that danger is looming. The person then chooses to either fight or flight, the psychological term given to the choices one can make when confronted with danger.

The capacity to be afraid is a normal and necessary function of the brain. The lack of fear, not the presence of fear, denotes a neurological problem. Some Christian people I counselled over the years have suffered with guilt because of their fear; they sincerely believed it to be a sin. However, the supposition that there should never be fear or doubt or confusion is a false one that too many Christians base their beliefs upon. We are human, and a part of our condition is to know fear, confusion, and doubt. We are wounded people; we have flaws, we have messed up lives, and we are all in need of a Savior. It is only as we put simple trust in the Lord that we can be whole. Fear is real, but there are some things we need to understand about fear to be able to deal appropriately with this emotion.

I am encouraged by the many accounts in the Bible that deal with this topic. Joshua 1 is the promise of God to be with His people through their challenges. God repeats His promise to them again and again, and we read, "Be strong and courageous, because you will lead these people to the land I swore to their ancestors to give them" (Joshua 1:6), followed by Joshua 1:7: "Be strong and very courageous," and again in Joshua 1:9, "Have I not commanded you? Be strong and courageous. Do not be afraid; do not be discouraged, for the Lord your God will be with you wherever you go." God understands the human proclivity to fear, and that is why He reminds His people not to be afraid. God's command not to be afraid does not mean the eradication or absence of fear, but the subjection of fear to simple trust. Why? For one simple reason: He is with us.

So let's try to understand fear and how we respond to this emotion.

- Fear is at times instinctive and vital for the avoidance of danger. When people sense danger approaching, then fear is a necessary emotion, enabling them to respond appropriately. However, some fears are not real but imaginary. In other words, we can fear the unknown or be terrified by what might happen. Or put another way, fear is a figment of the mind. Other fears come from associations; if you or someone you know had a motor accident, you could legitimately feel afraid to drive in a car. Fear is real, and it is not a sin, unless left unchecked and never confronted. Fear can be a friend. If you are functioning as you should, then a dangerous situation presenting itself will send the correct signals to those parts of the brain that respond to stress, and you will act promptly and appropriately. In this case, the emotion of fear is a friend. However, it is important to note that this is specific to the situation; fear should not be a consistent part of our lives.

- Fear must be confronted. Today, we read the story about Nehemiah, who was a cupbearer to King Artaxerxes. He was living in the city of Susa, in Persia (modern-day Iran), and longed to get back to Jerusalem, the city of his ancestors. He needed to request permission from the king, and he was, in the words of the Bible, "very much afraid" (Nehemiah 2:2). Nehemiah had a dream to go back to Jerusalem and rebuild the walls of the city, but he understood the gravity of standing before the king and requesting permission to leave. He realized that his petition could be denied, or more sobering, the king, if dissatisfied with him or his request, could order his execution. The point of this story is that although Nehemiah was afraid, his fear did not hold him back. Nehemiah confronted his fear and made fear a friend, not a foe. He went before the king and boldly presented his request to him, despite his insides quivering and his knees shaking. He refused to let fear control him.
- Fear can dictate your actions and determine your future. If Nehemiah had bowed to his fear, he would never have

gone back to Jerusalem and built the walls of the city. His entire future and the future of his people would have been jeopardized and limited by his choices. What Nehemiah did was confront his fear. He did not allow anxiety to stop him; rather, he let it propel him into a preferred future. I encourage you to take time to read the book of Nehemiah to fully understand how he dealt with fear.

Over and again, the Bible exhorts us to not fear. Have you noted what usually follows the words that we should not be afraid? Most times in the biblical text, the statement that follows on its heels tells us that God will be with us: "for the Lord your God will be with you wherever you go" (Joshua 1:9).

We do not have to fear any situation, any event, the future, or anything else because God will be with us. All we need is simple trust to take Him at His word.

I have had to deal with fear in my life. There were times that fear would get its tentacles around my thoughts, holding them in its tenacious grip, seeking to squeeze out every ounce of trust from me. But in those moments, I reminded myself of God's promise to be with me and to walk with me through my situation. He has never failed. I know He never will. All He asks of you today is that you put your simple trust in Him. Be strong and courageous because you know your God is with you.

Reflection

Tell God about your fears. Write them down on this page. Now look at those fears and speak to them; say, "I will not let fear hold me back from accomplishing what God has for me. I refuse to allow fear to control me." Now write down a Bible verse that you can take with you into this week. Memorize that verse and keep repeating it throughout the day. When fear comes knocking on the door, remind yourself that God is with you, and hold fast to His promise.

 Prayer

God, I give You my fear. I acknowledge it before You. You have promised that You will be with me, and I take You at Your word. I hold to the truth of Your word today and believe You will go before me and guide me and help me. I choose to lay my fear at Your feet. Your promises are sure, and I know that You are with me. Please give me courage for all that I will face today.

How to Handle Criticism

 Reading: Job 6

I do not like being criticized, but I know that at times, it has produced good in me. Of course, it is largely dependent upon how I respond to that criticism, but if I have the appropriate response, I am usually able to grow and become a better person. If you live long enough, you will be criticized about something. It may be as minor as the clothes you wear, or it may attack the core of who you are, but as certainly as the sun comes up tomorrow, you will experience criticism.

Can you imagine if we only received praise and affirmation all the days of our lives? We would be narcissistic human beings, which would make us most unattractive. So criticism is not always a negative ordeal, depending on how we respond to it.

Of course, when we want to talk about criticism, we need go no further than the book of Job. This man knew all about criticism. And the people heaping the criticism on him were his friends. Some friends, huh? I love what Job 6:24 says: "Teach me, and I will be quiet; show me where I have been wrong." What a wise and humble response to his critics.

There are three evaluations we need to make when we are being criticized:

- Evaluate the source of criticism. Where is the critique coming from? Is the source reliable and trustworthy? To be honest, there are some mean-spirited people in the world who live with the aim and purpose of criticizing anything that moves. I would not place value on their words. However, when the source is credible, even if the criticism stings, you need to stop and evaluate it. There are times when criticism from good people can help us to grow and become better people.

- Evaluate the truth of the criticism. Now, to do this, you have to be objective, and that is difficult when you feel you are being attacked. So don't take criticism too personally. You will never be able to evaluate the truth of the criticism if you feel hurt, are offended, or feel sorry for yourself. Ask yourself the question, is there truth to what is being said? If there is no truth in what is being said, then you need to discard the criticism. If there is some measure of truth in the words, then you need to assess what that piece of truth is. To do this takes immense strength of character, honesty, and humility. Job's response to his critics is prudent. He wants them to point out where he has gone wrong. He is not afraid to find out because he wants to learn and to grow.

- Evaluate yourself in the light of that criticism. Try to stand outside of the situation (yes, I know it's difficult) and evaluate the words being spoken. A Job response is, show me so that I can learn. Are there areas of your life that you need to deal with in the light of this criticism? Remember, if the criticism does not fit, do not wear it.

As tough as criticism can be, it can have value. Many lessons I've learned have been from my critics. Some of those people genuinely cared about me, but some did not. Surprisingly, I have even learned from the people who did not care about me. If you respond appropriately to criticism, you will become a better person. Whatever you do, do not allow criticism to make you angry or bitter. And avoid becoming introspective or down-hearted. Learn from it, grow through it, be thankful for it, and then forget it, and move forward. Dust yourself off, and start this day with enthusiasm and joy.

Reflection

Write down the people who are criticizing you and what they are saying. Carefully evaluate the truth of what is being said. Can you learn from any of it? Now pray for the person who is criticizing you, and allow your heart to be free of hurt and anger.

Prayer

God, I pray for those who are attacking me. I ask You to help me to evaluate carefully what is being said. Teach me the lessons I need to learn so I can become a better person. Help me to reflect You throughout this day. Help me to keep my spirit from anger and hurt, and to become everything that You want me to be.

How to Give Constructive Criticism

 Reading: Galatians 6:1–10

As we said in the previous devotion, no one revels in receiving criticism. I sometimes think that giving constructive criticism to a person is almost as difficult as receiving it is. However, most people are aware that if you are a living, moving human being, then you will receive criticism at some point in your life, and you will also need to challenge people as well. Some criticism is destructive, but some can help people to flourish and improve.

So how do we give criticism that can help people and not undermine or diminish their self-worth?

The Bible is a great place to start. It gives some sound advice for how to give criticism. Ephesians 4:15 says, "Instead, speaking the truth in love, we will grow to become in every respect the mature body of him who is the head, that is, Christ." There are five principles here that guide us when we have to critique someone:

- You should speak to people when they need confronting. The Bible exhorts us to speak honestly; in other words, you have to be verbal. There is nothing worse than walking away from people and talking behind their back. It is also unhelpful to give signals or roll your eyes or sigh. The most important task is determining that you will go and confront the person verbally.

- You should choose your moment and your words carefully. You can be kind, or you can be nice, as I discussed in an earlier devotion. And there is a difference. The Bible says we must be truthful when we confront someone. As you begin your constructive criticism, find some way you can affirm them before pointing out their flaw. This helps them to know they are valued, and they will probably consider what you say more carefully. Remember that your criticism might hurt, but it will inevitably help them.

  When you are confronting a person about an issue it is important to think carefully about the words you use. You may even want to write them down or say them aloud so that you can hear how they sound. Remember, you want your words to heal, not to harm. It is also important to choose the right moment to speak. There is a time to talk and a time to be quiet. Ecclesiastes 3 reminds us that there is a time for everything. If you choose the wrong time, your words could fall on fallow ground. Timing is everything.

- You should ensure your heart is right. You should never criticize somebody if you are angry because your words will not be helpful and could, in fact, be harmful. If you are deeply entrenched in the situation and feel angry with the one you plan to confront, then take pause. Give yourself time to think and to pray. Words that come from an angry heart can cause heartache. If your heart is right and your desire is to help the person and see them flourish, then only good can come from you speaking up.

- You should be clear and concise. Be precise with your words, and do not beat about the bush. The person you confront should understand what you are saying and know what needs to change. Remember, you want to help this person to grow and be better, so be clear about what you say. Focus on the issue, and don't meander down unnecessary paths.
- You should ensure there is a solution. You want to build people up; you don't want to demolish them. So make sure you go into the conversation with a complete understanding of what is at risk. In other words, have evidence for what you say, and be sure of the facts. Then ensure that there is a solution and that you can assist in finding a way through the problem. Be there to help and support the person through the issue. The conversation is just the first phase. Helping the person to the next phase is another process.

If you need to confront and critique someone, I urge you to pause, pray, plan an appropriate time to go and speak to the person, and then determine to be kind and yet truthful in what you say. Above all, ensure that your heart is right and that you want the best for the person you are confronting. If your words are loving and honest, they could propel that person into a bright future, or they could be a healing balm for some hurting soul. Your honest critique can set someone on a whole new trajectory that enables her or him to flourish.

Reflection

Think carefully about the person you will challenge. Write down what you will say. Read those words out aloud. Alter them if you must. Now go and do what you need to do with courage, love, and humility.

Prayer

God, I thank You for a new day and all the opportunities this day holds. I pray for wisdom to live and for boldness and grace to speak truthfully to someone today. Give me the courage I need to confront the person who needs to be challenged. May my words be kind but truthful, and let them result in healing.

A Joy-Filled Home

 Readings: Isaiah 32:16–20; Proverbs 3:33, 31:10–31

Paul and I had a lovely home in North Carolina that we decided to sell for practical reasons. We live and work in North Dakota, and so we were back in North Carolina less frequently, and keeping up with yard work was becoming arduous.

The day came to pack up our home and leave it after fourteen years. I felt sad as I walked through the empty house and thought of all the memories we had made in that two-story brick home. My heart was downcast, and I was thinking, *I am so sad to be leaving our home.* And as surely as I have ever heard God speak to me, I heard Him say, "You are leaving your house [the bricks and mortar], but you are taking your home with you." Wow. What a moment. I stopped in my tracks to consider those words. Yes, I was leaving the shell of my house behind, but all the wonderful, happy memories were going with me.

It is so important that we are committed to making our houses into joy-filled homes. These are some of the things I think are important:

- Talk and tell stories. When our family gathers around the dinner table, there is noise. Everyone is talking, and sometimes all at the same time. We love to tell stories from our past and stories about today. We sit and laugh and sometimes cry as we remember the wonderful and happy times in other places. We may have left those places years ago, but we wrapped up all our memories and stored them in our memory boxes to continuously draw them out at appropriate times to share them with each other. Some of the stories get told over and over, but they reinforce family, joy, gratitude, and love. Talk to each other, tell stories, and build great memories.

  It is also important to spend time talking about the Bible and the amazing stories in God's Word. I love what the book of Deuteronomy 6:6–9 says: "These commandments that I give you today are to be on your hearts. Impress them on your children. Talk about them when you sit at home and when you walk along the road, when you lie down and when you get up. Tie them as symbols on your hands and bind them on your foreheads. Write them on the doorframes of your houses and on your gates." As Christian families, the Bible narratives should be foundational to everything we do.

- Share meals together. Some families are too busy. Everyone is rushing in different directions, and we all have our own agenda. If you want to create a home full of joy and happiness, make time to eat together. There is nothing as enriching as sharing a meal with each other. You can sit around the table and share your burdens, difficulties, dreams, and joys. The meal table is a safe place for families to share their hearts. Don't disregard the importance of eating together. I know we live in a fast-paced world, and some people struggle to find time to even eat a meal, but we need to discipline ourselves to find time to share meals together.

- Pray together. Praying together as families is also important. Of course, we need our own prayer times, but we also need to pray together. Why not read a short passage or devotional together and then get a different family member to pray? When we go away on family vacations, we love our time of prayer and reflection in the evening. After our meal, we linger at the table and share some special memory from the day, and then everyone takes a turn to pray. Those have been some of the most meaningful and special times our family has shared.

- Celebrate together. Whenever there is a birthday, graduation, or a major milestone in the life of a family member, you should celebrate it. Fill the house with balloons, make a big cake, put the music on, and honor the person's achievement. Not every celebration needs to be lavish, but we do need to mark milestones.

- Play together. Don't pass each other like ships in the dark; do life with each other. We love to go away as a family, and when we do, we make amazing memories. Our grandchildren love spending time with us. They beg us to have sleepovers at our house, and we have fun. We read to them, play UNO and Monopoly with them, laugh together, go on long walks where they tell us about their dreams, and all round just enjoy each other's company. We are making memories that I hope they will take into their lives long after we have gone home to Jesus. One of the things our family loves to do is spend a week at the beach together directly after Christmas. We take long walks on the beach, play tennis and golf, swim and eat and play way too much UNO. We have the best times ever. We play hard, laugh hard, and love hard.

So where was I? Yes, I was telling you about leaving my little house. I walked out of my beautiful house and packed up all my memories, storing them carefully in my mind, and I knew everything was going to be okay. I was moving to a new residence that would quickly become a home filled with joy, new memories, and all the wonderful stories that I was taking with me. Don't let your home be a place where you simply sleep; let it be a place where you make wonderful, beautiful, and lasting memories with each other, a safe place where you find peace and joy.

Reflection

What can you do to make your home a place that is filled with joy? Think about different ways you can do this. Write down your plans to sit down and have meals together on certain days. Think about and write down the different things you can do over the holidays to make some special memories. Now go and start filling your home with joy.

Prayer

God, fill our home with joy and love. Help me to make my home a place where we can make beautiful memories. I want it to be filled with peace as well as joy. Enable me to do everything I can to make my home a place where everyone wants to be.

Dealing with Disappointment and Despondency

 Reading: Luke 24

The story in Luke 24 is in some way a sad story that reflects the deep disappointment the disciples experienced after Jesus's crucifixion. The One on Whom all their hopes were pinned had died a gruesome death, and the world appeared doomed by sin with no hope. It seemed that Satan had triumphed.

This story has many layers to it. It begins with the women taking the spices they had prepared for Jesus's body to the tomb. When they arrive at the tomb, they find his body has disappeared, and the tomb is empty. Angels assure the frightened women that Jesus had risen from the dead, but when the women told the disciples the news, they thought they were talking nonsense. Impetuous Peter ran to the tomb to see if Jesus's body had disappeared, and when he got there, he saw only strips of linen where the Lord had previously lain. It's all there in this chapter.

The narrative continues with two of the disciples walking on the road to Emmaus; their faces are downcast, and their hearts are sad. All hope seemed lost. But that was certainly not the reality; it was only how it seemed to the disciples. The truth was that hope was filling the world in a new and eternal way, and the world would never be the same again. The chapter continues with Jesus revealing Himself to His disciples and then concludes with His ascension to heaven. It really is a story textured in loss, grief, surprise, joy, and hope.

I can recall a time in our lives when all hope seemed lost. Paul and I had just had a major disappointment, and we were both reeling from it. We wondered where God was in all our plans and future. Our hearts felt hopeless. We thought we would never understand what had happened or why God had allowed it. In all of my adult life, I had not experienced such a deep disappointment. So I can empathize with those two disciples on the Emmaus road. All their hopes had been dashed. Their Messiah had died on a cruel Roman gibbet, and their world had been turned upside down. To them at that moment, all hope was gone.

I felt as if I had nowhere to turn. I did not feel the liberty to share my disappointment with anyone, and so I threw myself on God.

When all hope seems lost, remember that Easter is on the way. As the saying goes, "It's Friday, but Sunday is coming." The disciples had not realized that Jesus had risen, as He said He would. I felt like those disciples; I couldn't even imagine Easter as part of my future, but even as darkness enshrouded my soul, God was looking on my situation completely differently. If you experienced a disappointment (or someone you know has), here are a few principles to help you to navigate your discouragement:

- God has the final word. Jesus's disciples only understood a part of the story. I had only seen a glimpse of my story. God was still at work in ways I could not comprehend, and the end of my seemingly hopeless story was a bright and wonderful ending, too wonderful for me to even contemplate. These two disciples were despondent and filled with disappointment. Although their perceptions were powerful, they were wrong. It was not the Jewish people, who committed Jesus to death on a cross, who had the final word; it was God. And His final word was resurrection.

- God can make something beautiful out of the ashes of life. I looked at the ashes of the events at my feet and wondered if anything good could come from this dismal event; it had colored my world with hopelessness. Yet God took those ashes and made something good. Yes, He is the only One Who can take the brokenness of our lives and make something magnificent. Jesus's death was terrible, bloody, and painful, but God defeated death, and Jesus rose from the grave to bring life and hope to a needy world. Listen to what Isaiah 61:3 says: "And provide for those who grieve in Zion—to bestow on them a crown of beauty instead of ashes, the oil of joy instead of mourning, and a garment of praise instead of a spirit of despair." God can replace your despair with joy and adorn you with a garment of praise, even in the midst of your despondency.

- God is in absolute control of our lives, even when we don't feel that He is. As I have already stated, I now realize that faith has little to do with my feelings. When I felt hopeless, God had everything in control. My feelings do not affect the authority and power of my God. He is God. When Paul was writing to the Colossian church, he told them, "He is before all things, and in Him all things hold together" (Colossians 1:17). You may feel as if everything is coming undone. It may appear that the stitches of the fabric of your life are unravelling, but be assured, God is still holding everything together. The world sometimes appears to be spinning out of control, but again the words of the apostle assure us that God holds everything together. Our trust is not in the political leaders who rule from seats of power in Washington, Downing Street, the Kremlin, or anywhere else; our trust is in the eternal God Who holds everything together.

Let hope seep into your soul today. When everything seems lost, remember God is still working and putting the pieces of the puzzle of your life together. We only see a part of the picture, but God sees everything; His perspective is an eternal one.

What those two disciples did not realize on the Emmaus road that day was that Christ had risen, and the future of the world was bright and full of hope. Despite their feelings of gloom and despair, the reality was that Jesus was there with them, even though they didn't recognize him. Even if you feel despondent and disappointed, the reality is that Jesus is walking right beside you, as He did with those two disciples so long ago.

Reflection

Pen your disappointment, writing down as many sentences as you need to. Open your heart to God, and tell Him exactly how you feel. Now remind yourself of the story you read of the two disappointed disciples on the Emmaus road. Remind yourself that although their perspective was powerful, it was wrong. Jesus was not dead. He was alive. Write down two ways in which you can focus on hope today.

Prayer

God, my heart is sad with disappointment, but I acknowledge Your presence, and I know that You are right here with me. I cannot feel You, but I know You are here. More importantly, I know that You hold everything together. You are eternal. You knew about today, and You know about tomorrow, so all I need to do is put my simple trust in You. Help me today to do precisely that. Let hope seep into every part of my soul. Let my focus be on You today, and help me to see things from Your eternal perspective and not my limited human one.

Don't Give People
Permission to Hurt You

 Reading: Psalm 139

I was standing at the kitchen sink, my hands in soapy water, washing grimy dishes. The view outside my window was magnificent. I gazed across our deck and into the yard filled with Australian gum trees, colorful parakeets perched in their branches, and the scent of the eucalyptus trees filtering through my windows. The sky was inky blue, and the sun filled the room with light.

My mood certainly did not match the radiance of the day. I was feeling down in the dumps as I thought about a couple in our congregation whose full-time occupation, it seemed, was to find fault in people and to point out everything that was wrong in our church. They had been particularly critical of Paul and me, and I was feeling despondent.

Complaining to the Lord, I asked Him, "How could ... be so critical, unkind, and claim to be Your disciples?" At that time, we were pastoring a large church in Australia, working hard, doing our best, and all this couple could do was focus on what they perceived was wrong. The other problem was that they seemed to enjoy filling as many people's ears as they possibly could with their criticisms. That was when I heard a voice in my head that I instinctively knew was the Lord speaking to me.

He said, "Don't give them permission to hurt you."

I almost said, "I beg your pardon, Lord?" I knew God had spoken to my heart because the words were powerful and seemed to penetrate my soul. I stopped washing the dishes and pondered the words God had said and what they really meant.

I realized how much import I placed on the words that other people spoke. In this case, I had allowed this criticism to enter my heart and to wound my spirit. I contemplated what God had said to me and recognized I had given these people permission to hurt me.

So here is what I learned that day:

- Only give trusted people access to your life. You are the guardian of your soul, and you can choose what you allow to enter your soul. Don't give people permission to access that most private aspect of your life. Of course, there are times when we need to heed the words of people, but they must be good people, trustworthy, and full of integrity, or their words are not worth heeding. I considered this couple who were criticizing us and realized they were not living lives that I respected. I did not trust them, and neither did I consider them people of integrity. So why was I allowing them to hurt me so deeply? I thought about their words for a moment and realized there was no truth to what they were saying, so why give heed to the words of people I neither respected nor trusted?
- Don't allow unkind words to gain space in your heart. It is amazing how powerful words are. Affirming and unkind words can play on our minds, and they can go around and around your head. When that happens, those words

can impact your spirit, and they can become of part of you and start to define who you are. Not all words have that effect, but the more prominent the person is in your life, the more meaning those words will have. You have to make a conscious decision that unkind words with no substance will not enter your soul. Yes, I know this is easier said than done. However, once you have considered what has been said and know it is not true, you have to decide to let those words go. You have to be disciplined not to ponder those words and give them free access to run down the corridors of your mind. If those words were critical and unkind, then the best thing you can do is to ignore what was said. Just make the decision that you will not allow lies and untruths to access your heart and find a resting place there.

- Don't build up walls around your heart. Sometimes, after people hurt us, we put up walls so that we can defend ourselves from further pain. That is an impossibility because in the course of our lives, we are bound to encounter criticism and unkindness of some sort or another. When we put up walls, we might think we protect ourselves from mean-spirited people, but the truth is, those walls are a barrier to kind and gracious people as well. We need to keep our hearts open, and we don't do that by putting up barriers. When you close your heart because of hurt, you also close your heart to the depth of meaning and beauty in authentic relationships. Choose not to dwell on past hurts. Don't keep peeling off the scab and making the wound bleed again. Never waste your time thinking about people who have hurt you; they do not deserve that space in your heart and mind. Make wise choices on a daily basis, and only allow people you love and trust to access those private spaces of your life.

- Determine not to be robbed of your joy. Today is a new day, and you need to decide that it will be a good one. I have already alluded to the fact that being joyful is a choice we can make, even when circumstances seem joyless. It amazes me how susceptible I have been to people and how many times I allowed them to rob me of my joy. But as I have grown in my walk with the Lord, I have realized that true and lasting joy is found in Jesus. God loves you, my friend. I assure you that the unkind words that have been spoken over your life are not words that you would hear from God. You are His child, and He wants your life to be abundant in every way. You may have encountered some unkind people along the way, but there are also many good and kind people out there. God is a good and faithful God, so when people fail you, remind yourself that the Lord will never fail or betray you.

There are times when a mentor, friend, parent, or trusted leader speaks into our lives, and we need to listen. Sometimes, what they say is honest but harsh, and we have to heed those words for our own benefit. We cannot expect only affirmation throughout our lives. Sometimes, we need words of warning or correction or rebuke, and those words, if heeded, will make us better human beings. Words of correction are necessary for our own growth and development as healthy and well-balanced humans. Those are not the words I have been discussing today. I have been talking about words that are malicious and meant to harm you. Those words should never gain access to your soul.

Reflection

Consider the reading for today; God formed you. He knows you and all your thoughts; He hems you in, and His hand is on you.

What rich content and deep truths in these verses. Let the truth seep into your heart and remind yourself that God made you, and He loves you. Now write down the most meaningful verse in this psalm and memorize it so you can mull over the truth of those words throughout this day.

Prayer

God, I am so thankful that You love me and that I am Your child. I pray that You will enable me to let go of some of the words that have been spoken over my life. Help me not to mull them over in my brain, but to rather consider the truths in Your Word. Assist me in letting go of the hurt that words have caused me, and let my relationship with You flourish as I consider Your amazing, unconditional love for me.

Breaking Bad Habits

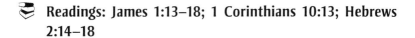

📖 **Readings: James 1:13–18; 1 Corinthians 10:13; Hebrews 2:14–18**

If we are honest with ourselves, and that is not always easy, we have all struggled with a bad habit at some stage of our lives. Some habits are so ingrained in our brain that we do things without even thinking. In other words, the habit has become second nature to us; those habits can be destructive to our own souls and aggravating or annoying to others.

Of course, there are some habits that are good, and we should constantly work at acquiring good behavior patterns. However, today we are focusing on destructive behavior patterns that whittle away at our self-worth, relationships, and our overall well-being.

Bad habits can be problems with food, alcohol, drugs, sex, pornography, and the list goes on. So how do we break bad habits?

- Be honest with yourself. You have to arrive at the place in your life where you acknowledge that this habit is destructive. You may think that you can control your habit, but can you really? You will never break a habit if you cannot be honest about your own weakness and the powerful and destructive nature of your habit. Look deep within yourself and ask yourself if this is how you want to live your life. After you do this, you need to confess your weakness to God and ask Him for help.

- Be honest about the influencers in your life. Is there a person who is encouraging this destructive force in your life? Now, don't get me wrong here. I am not asking you to play the blame game. But it is necessary to identify people who are enabling you. In other words, there are some people who are not going to help you to break this pattern in your life, and you need to be honest and admit that so you limit their influence in your life. 1 Corinthians 15:33–34 says, "Do not be misled: Bad company corrupts good character. Come back to your senses as you ought, and stop sinning; for there are some who are ignorant of God—I say this to your shame." There may be people you need to break your connection with because they are not helping you live the kind of life you should be living.
- Consider tomorrow. Before you go rushing into some destructive habit, give tomorrow some consideration. There may be momentary pleasure in what you are doing in the moment, but tomorrow will be a different matter altogether. What you do today has real and lasting consequences for tomorrow.
- Surround yourself with good people. As much as bad company corrupts good character, so too does good company help to create upright character. If you have a problem with alcohol, you do not want to be in the company of people who drink and encourage you to do the same. Find good people who will surround you with support and make you accountable for your behavior. Make sure you are part of a community of people where you hear good Bible teaching and have wholesome friendships. When you are in church, you are surrounded by other people who are

striving to live lives that honor and please God. Remember that the Lord is there for you. He does not condemn you; He reaches out to you so you can find wholeness and healing. Read 1 Corinthians 10:13 again and remind yourself that God will help you in your temptation.

- Don't give in to disillusionment. You may fail and fall, but that doesn't mean you give up. Get up, shake the dust off, and start again. Go easy on yourself. Don't be ashamed to ask for help from trusted friends or church leaders. Never try to do this journey solo because we were never meant to go it alone. We all need support in our Christian walk, and we need each other to succeed.

Your habit took time to develop, and it will take time to form new behaviours. I am not pretending that this is going to be an easy journey, but it will be a worthwhile one. Ask anyone who has broken a debilitating habit if she or he would choose to go back to that destructive behaviour; the answer will be a resounding no.

(&) Reflection

Write down what habit you are seeking to break. Now read over what you have written. Write down three steps you can take to break this destructive force in your life. Try to memorize one of the scripture readings from today. When temptation comes, you can draw on that verse and gain strength from it.

(prayer-icon) Prayer

God, I acknowledge my weakness before You. I ask unashamedly for Your help in this area of my life. I long to know and experience freedom from bondage. I come to You today seeking help and assistance with this habit and asking You to give me the victory.

Identifying
the Pharisee in Me

 Reading: Matthew 7

As a young person, I assumed from my readings of the Bible that Pharisees were awful people. Jesus seemed to be at loggerheads with them at all times, and my assumption was that they were despicable, judgmental, and unkind.

As I read my Bible over the years, I realize I gave the Pharisees a harder rap than I should have. They were evidently devout people who tried their best to be good and attempted to do what was right. But that was precisely what the problem was; they focused entirely on their own efforts and their personal goodness, and somewhere, God was lost in all their religious paraphernalia.

Jesus constantly rebuked the Pharisees, but not because he despised them or rejected everything they did. No. Jesus loved the Pharisees and longed to see them freed from their religious bondage to serve God with pure hearts. They tried to be good, but they didn't know what it meant to be holy.

I started to look at the Pharisees, and I hang my head in shame and confess that some of their sins were mine (and some still are).

I have to work every day to dispel the Pharisaic tendencies in my own heart. What was it about the Pharisees that displeased Jesus?

- They saw everyone's faults and flaws. Have you ever been like that? Conscious of the failures of others and oblivious to the weakness in your own life? We have to try to keep our focus on Jesus and ask Him to give us patience as He works in the lives of others, while not forgetting that we need Him to work in our hearts as well. We have to remember that everyone has their own personal walk with the Lord, and for each one, the challenges are different. God equips us to run our own race, and others have a grace for the race they are on.

- They judged people who were not like them. They despised Gentiles, Samaritans, and anyone weak or disabled or sinful. In their view, weakness and sickness was a sign of God's judgment. If you were not like them, you were cast out. Sometimes, it is easy to judge people who are not like us or who are battling in areas we cannot imagine ever struggling with. We need to show people compassion and not pass judgment on those unlike us. Jesus was loving and accepting of all people everywhere.

  Consider the story of the Samaritan woman in John 4. When you read this narrative, you are struck by the fact that Jesus was challenging two of the prevailing cultural assumptions of the day. Jesus, the rabbi, spoke to a woman, and this was strictly against the code of the religious Jew. She was also a Samaritan, a despised racial group that any religious Jew avoided. Yet in this conversation with her, Jesus challenges racism and sexism. He doesn't preach against the issues; he doesn't put up placards and scream on street corners. No, He shows love and compassion, and speaks lovingly to a deeply despised Samaritan woman, and in so doing challenges these two pervasive beliefs in society. Jesus, unlike the Pharisees, demonstrated His love by the way He lived and treated others.

- They said one thing and did another. Jesus often challenged the Pharisees about their inconsistencies. Yes, they would pray daily, they gave of their tithes, but their actions towards people who were different from them were unkind and harsh. The story of the good Samaritan in Luke 10 is telling. It is the story of three people, two of whom were religious. Yet the two religious people, the priest and Levite, would not stoop down to help a man stripped and beaten, lying on the side of the road, about to die. It was the Samaritan man (despised by the religious elite) who went over to the wounded man and bandaged his injuries, took him to an inn, and paid for all his needs.

  Sometimes, it is too inconvenient for me to cross over to the other side of the road and get involved in the needs of someone hurting. There are times I just do not like to get my hands dirty. Jesus challenged this lack of compassion in the Pharisees, and I know He also challenges those tendencies in my heart. Sometimes, it is easy to throw money at some organization or at some institution because getting involved personally could just get messy.

I recognize that there are elements of the Pharisee in my heart that must be dealt with. I want to love all people everywhere, regardless of their color, creed, nationality, or anything else, for that matter. Jesus loved all people everywhere. I also want to live in a way that reveals the magnificent Jesus, Who has been so patient and loving with me. I want to love like He does, to shine in a dark world and bring the hope of Christ into desperate situations. I want to deal a death blow to the Pharisee in me that always seems to surface at the most unlikely moments. I want

Jesus to shine through my life so that others will see His beauty and be drawn to Him.

Reflection

Write down the names of one or two people you have felt inclined to judge. Now write down how you can begin to pray for these people, and ask God to guide you to pray specific prayers over their lives.

Prayer

God, help me to deal with the Pharisee inside my own heart. I pray that I would see people through Your eyes. There is so much vitriol and hatred in our world, and I want Your kingdom to come on earth. Use me to show love and kindness to people who are different from me. Help me to have patience with those who are still working through issues in their lives that I cannot understand. Above all, I pray for grace and love for people everywhere.

When God Messes
with Our Plans

 Reading: Isaiah 55

I can still feel the confusion and despondency that ran through every fiber of my being, the sick feeling in the pit of my stomach. *How could this possibly be?* I asked myself. Our plans were coming together, things were working out, and our future looked bright. And best of all, our plans seemed to have the fingerprint of God upon them. Suddenly, *boom,* they vanished in a cloud of dust.

Have you ever had a dream, a desire, a goal that has suddenly come to nothing? You were dreaming of a bright future; you could smell success, adventure filled your veins, and you were infused with passion for a bright new season. And then someone else got the promotion or the sale fell through or there was a sudden tragic event that halted your plan or an unexpected illness stopped you in your tracks. All these and other extenuating circumstances can mess with our dreams, our plans, and the longings and desires of our hearts.

So here is what I learned as I reflected on some of the shattered plans of my life (and there have been a few of them):

- God knows and sees what I cannot know or see. God is infinitely more clever than I am. He is also eternal, and He sees what I cannot see. I might be aware of all the circumstances of my life, but God alone knows the future. We have to rest in the truth that God sees the big picture that I cannot see. I want to highlight these verses from our reading today, found in Isaiah 55:8–9: "'For my thoughts are not your thoughts, neither are your ways my ways,' declares the Lord. 'As the heavens are higher than the earth, so are my ways higher than your ways and my thoughts than your thoughts.'" God sees things from an eternal perspective, whereas our view is a limited one. This is why we can rest in God's ways because He knows and sees what we cannot.
- God is revealing His love and mercy. I have sometimes felt that God was right in the center of the plans we were making. He was there with us, guiding us and leading us on the journey. Then the plan got messed up and left us with a heap of rubble at our feet. In those moments, I have been confused and devastated, but I know enough about my God to know that His plans are infinitely greater than ours. I know He is a good God and does not desire harm for me or my family. So in those moments, I run to Him and cast myself on Him, and I mean I throw myself on His mercy. You see, I do believe that God is merciful, and that is the only reason He messes with our plans. He knows the things I do not know. He sees the circumstances ahead of me. He is aware of the path I aim to take and the stumbling blocks along that road.

Hebrews 4:16 says, "Let us then approach God's throne of grace with confidence, so that we may receive mercy and find grace to help us in our time of need." You can approach God with confidence and know that He will hear your cry and extend His gracious hand of mercy towards you. Be assured that He will never turn you away, no matter what your faults or flaws. He is always there to help us in our time of need. As difficult as it can be to comprehend, let me remind you of this truth: "And we know that in all things, God works for the good of those who love him, who have been called according to his purpose" (Romans 8:28). My friend, all things, even those situations that seem inexplicable and hurtful, can and will work for good in your life.

- God has a greater purpose for our lives. From this perspective in time, I see that He had a better plan. In times of confusion, I have to lay my dreams down. Yes, it is difficult, especially when you've been filled with a particular dream, day and night. Now that dream is smashed, and you must pick up the broken pieces and move on. No, it is not easy. However, I remind myself that He must have something significantly greater in His plan for my life. I remind myself that my plans are often different from God's plans. Part of trusting the Lord, as Proverbs 3:5 says, means, "lean not on your own understanding." That is difficult for me. Sometimes, my own thoughts make far more sense to me than God's way. There are even times I think what God is doing is illogical because I use my limited perspective and understanding of the situation. I see things from a human perspective, God sees everything from an eternal one, and so I must trust Him because He knows best.

- God's purpose will come to pass if we trust Him. I have seen people become bitter with the Lord because of their disappointment. Their messed-up plans lead them to question Him, and some have even lost their faith. In these trying times, we have to guard our hearts carefully and remind ourselves of some of the eternal truths I have been addressing: God loves us; He does not want to hurt us. God is trustworthy; He has a better plan than the one we have. God's timing is different from ours; He has an eternal perspective

So if you are like me, you have felt the agonizing sense of loss and disappointment when your plan failed, when God messed with your dreams and desires. But if you focus on His mercy, love, kindness, and faithfulness, you will understand that He has something far better for you in the future. You may not see it now; it may take some time, but you will see and experience His goodness. Be encouraged by Isaiah 55:10–12: "As the rain and the snow come down from heaven, and do not return without watering the earth and making it bud and flourish, so that it yields seed for the sower and bread for the eater, so is my word that goes out from my mouth: It will not return to me empty, but will accomplish what I desire and achieve the purpose for which I sent it. You will go out in joy and be led forth in peace; the mountains and the hills will burst into song before you, and all the trees of the field will clap their hands." Take courage, and put simple trust in a God Who knows best and wants you to flourish.

Reflection

In your own words, express to God what is in your heart today. Let Him know your dreams and plans. Now put those plans in His hands, and ask Him to lead and guide you.

Prayer

God, You know the end from the beginning. My plans appear to have come to nothing, but I know that You have my future securely in Your hands. I know that I can trust You because You are a merciful and loving God. Reassure my heart of Your love for me and help me to rest in Your perfect plan for my life and place simple trust in You.

Taking Action or
Trusting God

 Reading: Psalm 62

Oh boy, I have faced situations in my life when I ask myself the question, what do I do in this position I find myself in? Do I sit back and trust God, or do I manipulate circumstances and lend God a hand? In other words, do I take action, or do I trust God?

Well, I think we should do both. We have considered this text a number of times in this book, but it warrants our attention again. Look at Proverbs 3:5–6: "Trust in the Lord with all your heart and lean not unto your own understanding; in all your ways submit to him, and he will make your paths straight." There is sound advice in those verses. We need to trust God absolutely and with our entire beings. And we are not to lean on our own understanding.

I do a lot of that; I tell God I want to trust Him completely, but then the gears of my finite mind start turning, and my brain goes into overdrive, and I suggest to God all the wonderful and ingenious ways I think He could answer my prayer. As if God needs my help or my suggestions. God often surprises me by how

He answers my requests. Most of the time, He does things in ways I never anticipated. Psalm 62:8 says, "Trust in him at all times, you people; pour out your hearts to him, for God is our refuge." In every situation of life, we need to have that simple trust on all occasions, in a God Who is our refuge.

So where is the balance between trusting God and taking action in the situation? Let me share a few thoughts that have helped me in my journey:

- When confronted with an impossible situation, spend extra time in prayer. If I am at a crossroads or facing a situation that seems out of control from a human standpoint (and I have faced many), I set aside extra time in my day for prayer. Our text exhorts us to open our hearts and tell God everything. I sometimes skip a meal and use that time for earnest prayer. The word *earnest* used by the praying church in Acts 12 is the same earnestness with which Jesus prayed in the Garden of Gethsemane. It is the kind of earnestness when you are deeply moved and compelled to pray. So over and above my daily devotion, I call upon God at particular times in the day to hear my prayer and to meet the need.

- When confronted with an impossible situation, recall the times God has done the impossible. I have seen God do the impossible over and over, so I have faith buried in the deep crevices of my heart that I draw upon in moments like this. I literally walk down the corridors of my mind, search in each room, and bring out the stories of God's faithfulness and goodness in my life. I dwell on them and speak about them so as to remind my own heart that I serve a faithful God. In Deuteronomy 6, God commands the people of Israel to tell their children about the miracles He did for them. They are encouraged to talk about them when they sit at home and when they walk on the road or lie on their bed, constantly reminding themselves of God's faithfulness. These reminders will inspire our hearts to pray earnestly in the midst of difficulties. Our text today reminds us that power belongs to God. And we need to instil in our thinking that God is omnipotent and that He can do the impossible.

- When confronted with an impossible situation, do everything you can. Don't just sit on your laurels and say, "Okay, God, if You are omnipotent, show me your power." You have to do everything you can in the circumstances. So let me explain what I mean here, because it might sound as if I am being contradictory by saying trust God and do everything you can in the situation. If you need a job, you pray about it, but you also send out resumes and do all you can on your part to get a job. Yes, you trust God implicitly, but you don't just sit and do nothing. You need to take some action in the situation. If I am praying to be at the top of my field, I can trust God to open up doors, but I also need to work and study and be intentional in doing all I can to answer my own prayer. It doesn't diminish faith; it adds to the element of trust. With everything I do to see the answers to my prayers, I still need God to come through in the situation. I have to add that most times, I am surprised by the way God answers my prayer.

The conclusion of our reading today reminded us that God is omnipotent and that we will all be rewarded according to the works that we have accomplished. God rewards our faith and our actions, and when we combine the two together, they make a powerful combination.

So when it comes to trusting God, it is simple trust, but it also requires us to do our part. God works with us in accomplishing His plan and purpose. Try to put aside some extra time for earnest prayer. Remind yourself of God's faithfulness by reading stories from the Bible and even stories of men and women of faith who have proved God in their lives. Finally, do everything you can to ensure that you do your part in answering your prayer.

Reflection

Write down what actions you can take in your situation. Contemplate how you can set aside some extra time for prayer. What extra steps can you take in the circumstance surrounding you? Read this psalm again and remind yourself that God is a faithful God.

Prayer

God, I trust You with the situation I find myself in. Give me wisdom to know what action I should take in this instance. Give me grace and peace as I wait patiently for You to answer my prayer. I choose to put my simple trust in You today.

Seven Principles
for Soul Care

 Reading: Psalm 1

When we left our homeland in South Africa to move to the beautiful city of Brisbane, Australia, our family was filled with excitement and apprehension.

One of our poignant memories of South Africa was the beautiful jacaranda trees in the springtime. The blaze of color that filled our city streets when the trees blossomed in September was a sight for sore and hungry eyes. We were delighted to discover that there was a plethora of these subtropical trees in Brisbane. As the city awakens from its winter slumber, the jacaranda trees shower the streets and paths with the most beautiful purple blossom. The trees form a canopy of mauve that is almost impossible to adequately describe, and their trumpet-shaped petal gives off a subtle fragrance, delighting the senses and heralding a new season.

When our son Jason was fourteen, he sent his grandparents a postcard of the tree-lined streets of Brisbane, with their mauve canopy adorning the sky, hoping that the indigo blossoms would help persuade them to come and join us in this beautiful city. I knew from his postcard that Jay's soul was prospering, and as a mother, the greatest joy you can feel is when your kids' souls are doing well.

In 3 John 1:2, we read, "Dear friend, I pray that you may enjoy good health and that all may go well with you, even as your soul is getting along well." I love this seemingly insignificant little verse where John writes to his dear friend Gaius and prays that his soul is doing well.

All of us want to lead successful lives, but how do we do we manage our souls to ensure that they prosper and remain healthy? There are seven principles we need to apply to our lives to sustain a healthy soul. I trust you will find them useful:

- Personal discipline. There are three important areas where we need to apply discipline in our lives. The first is that we need to make our souls accountable to God. This is a daily discipline we need to practice. Morning by morning, we take time out to open our hearts to God and make our souls accountable to Him. Psalm 1:2 says, "But whose delight is in the law of the Lord, and who meditates on his law day and night." This is possibly the most important discipline we can introduce into our lives to ensure a healthy soul. Take time to be in God's presence. The second one is to educate our souls. Proverbs 19:2 says, "Desire without knowledge is not good—how much more will hasty feet miss the way." Begin by educating your soul in God's Word; this is the most important knowledge to acquire. Read the Bible every day and let it shape your life as you apply the principles on a daily basis. You should also read good books and grow your knowledge by learning from the lives of others. The third is to refresh your soul. Ensure that you feed both your emotional and spiritual sides. We are often good at ensuring our spiritual tank stays full. We read our Bible, pray, go to church, and practice other disciplines that enhance our spiritual growth. However, some of us may not be aware of the importance of filling our emotional tanks. Filling your emotional tank is different from filling your spiritual one, and because we are all unique and have varying needs, the way we fill our tanks will be different for each person. I love to walk or sit quietly and read a book or watch a good movie. These are some of the ways in which I fill my emotional tank. Don't let your emotional tank run low because it will impact every part of your life.

- Pure hearts. I have mentioned several times that we are the guardians of our hearts. No one else can take care of your soul. We have to ensure that we work constantly at keeping our hearts clean. Proverbs 4:23 says, "Above all else, guard your heart, for everything you do flows from it." According to the writer of Proverbs, there is nothing more important than guarding your own heart. So then, we must ensure that no bitterness, anger, or unforgiveness grows in the soil of our souls.

- Praising lifestyles. Practice an attitude of gratitude, and be intentional about thanksgiving. Wake up and look around you and appreciate all you have and give God thanks. It is amazing how good it is for our souls to express appreciation to God and to others. Praise should never be dependent on how you feel. A lifestyle of praise means we thank God in the bad times as well as the good. It should be a part of the rhythm of our lives and a discipline ingrained into the flow of our existence.

- Proactive speech. The Bible gives us good advice with regard to our speech. Proverbs 13:3 says, "Those who guard their lips preserve their lives, but those who speak rashly will come to ruin." Jesus told us that what our hearts are full of will tumble out from our mouths. If your soul and heart are clean, then it follows that your words and speech will be pure. Make sure your words are life-giving. And don't define your life by the negative words spoken over you. Let me ask you a question: If you bump into a person with a glass full of milk, what do you get? Milk, of course. And everywhere. What do people get when they bump into you? What is in your heart will spill from your lips.

- Purposeful attitudes. God has put every one of us on this earth for a purpose. We need to discover that destiny and walk in it. Wake up with an "I can do anything" attitude, and see what God can do with your life. You have been placed on this earth for a reason; you have a destiny to fulfil. Start walking in that purpose today.

- People commitment. Matthew 28:19 instructs us, "Therefore go and make disciples of all nations, baptizing them in the name of the Father and of the Son and of the Holy Spirit, and teaching them to obey everything I have commanded you. And surely I am with you always, to the very end of the age." This is not a calling to a few chosen, but for every single person who loves Jesus. We must be prepared to share God's love with others. When we become introspective and selfish, our souls begin to atrophy, but as we look outward from ourselves and commit ourselves to others, then our own souls prosper at the same time.

- Positive outlook. Read Numbers 12–14 again to discover the detrimental impact of negative attitudes on an entire community. Negativity is contagious and can spread like wildfire. The story in Numbers is proof of that. We need to work constantly at ensuring a positive attitude and outlook.

These are the seven principles that we can put in place in our lives to ensure that our souls stay healthy. Be intentional about ensuring the health of your soul.

Reflection

Write down the important areas of your soul that you want to see prosper. What can you do to ensure the health of your soul?

 Prayer

God, I want my soul to prosper and to do well. Help me today to ensure that I put these simple principles in place in my life so that my soul will do well.

Don't Burn All Your Bridges

 Reading: Ephesians 4

A few years ago, my mom and dad spent ten weeks with us in the States, and it reminded me once again of the importance of family. My parents live in Perth, Australia, and so we do not see them on a regular basis. In fact, we count ourselves blessed if we can see them once in a year. We had a wonderful time with them; every day was special and filled with memories that we still revel in today. Saying goodbye was difficult because when your dad is in his nineties, and your mom close on his heels, there is a distinct possibility that you will not see them again, and believe me, that is really challenging.

Recently, a friend of mine lost one of her family members. It was a sad story of family feuds and disunity. It made me think of the incredible importance of our relationships. And yet some people will quickly discard a relationship or burn all their bridges because of an offense. Is it worth it? I think not, and here is why:

- Life is too short to have enemies. I cannot believe where time has gone. How is it that my passionate, fun-loving parents are now gray-haired and aged? Where did the years go? I remember my children playing in the sand and making mud pies, and now my grandchildren are doing those things. In fact, my grandchildren are already through the mud pie phase and are now into some deep and meaningful conversations with us. James 4:14 says, "You are a mist that appears for a little while and then vanishes." My friend, life on earth is short; there is no time to have enemies. It takes many years to build strong, healthy relationships, so there is never a good enough reason to extinguish any relationship over some offense. Our reading in Ephesians 4:26 says, "In your anger do not sin: Do not let the sun go down while you are still angry, and do not give the devil a foothold." When we hold grudges, we give the devil room in our lives. The Bible is wise when it exhorts us not to let anger or disagreement last for even a day. Before the sun sets on this day, deal with any issue at hand.

- Most disagreements are over trivialities. If you ask people who have not spoken to each other for many years, most of them cannot remember what the real issue was that caused the rift in their relationship. When they boil it all down, it is most times petty, and the offense has grown out of all proportions in their minds over the months and years. It is not grounded in reality. I understand there are situations that can be toxic and can cause rifts in relationships that are difficult to heal, but many times, this is not the case.

- Communication is the key to healing relationships. Most of our relationships fracture because of misunderstandings. Once you have been humble and courageous enough to confront the person, you realize how misunderstood you were or the other person was. That is why you need to talk. Don't play the silent game and stop talking, sending emails, or phoning. That type of behaviour never helps heal a situation or bring resolve. Open the discussion and ask, "Can we talk?" There is no place for pride in relationships; sometimes, you have to choose to be the bigger person. Our reading begins with a gentle exhortation: "Be completely humble and gentle; be patient, bearing with one another in love" (Ephesians 4:2). This verse is key to keeping our relationships healthy and strong. Humility, gentleness, and patience are vital to this process.

- Learn the power of the word *sorry*. Don't wait for the other person to say sorry; you take the initiative, and don't be surprised by the results. I have found the word *sorry* goes a long way in bringing reconciliation and healing in relationships. Our reading in Ephesians is pertinent, and the final verse in the chapter says, "Be kind and compassionate to one another, forgiving each other, just as in Christ God forgave you" (Ephesians 4:32). Forgiveness is foundational to the Gospel message, and just as we have been freely forgiven, so too do we need to practice forgiveness.

- Rebuilding a bridge can take a long time, so don't burn your bridge. Sometimes, hurts go deep, and some people wallow in self-pity to such an extent that even when they want to build a bridge back, it is impossible. So the lesson is, don't burn your bridges. In our reading, the aged apostle encourages us, "Make every effort to keep the unity of the Spirit through the bond of peace" (Ephesians 4:3). That is our task as Christ followers, and I encourage you to navigate your relationships with humility, gentleness, and patience.

If you are struggling with a relationship and are on the verge of burning all the bridges of the past, then this devotion is for you. Please take heed to what I have said. Life is too short to have even one enemy. It takes courage and humility to say, "Sorry," especially if you feel as if you are the wounded one, but I can assure you that it will be worth your while. Read the passage in Ephesians again, and ask God to clothe you with the virtues you need to bring resolve to your situation.

 ## Reflection

Is there someone you need to speak to today? Think carefully about what you will say, and write down the main points ahead of time.

 ## Prayer

God, I need Your help today. I ask You to give me the wisdom to continue to work on all my relationships. Help me to invest meaningfully in the people I love. Where there is stress in a relationship, give me sensitivity to know what to do and courage to do what I should.

Can I Really Do All Things through Christ?

 Reading: Philippians 4

I love the book of Philippians. It is full of encouragement and exhortation for our daily lives. What makes it such an exceptional epistle, in my view, is that when Paul wrote this letter, it was from his prison cell; conditions were dismal, and he was deprived of many of life's daily necessities. On top of all of that, he was not doing well physically. And yet, in the midst of discomfort, challenge, and struggle, he could still exhort and encourage the church in Philippi.

One of the well-known and oft-quoted verses in the Bible is found in Philippians 4:13: "I can do all this through him who gives me strength." However, it is probably one of the most misunderstood and misquoted verses in the New Testament. So let us consider a couple of principles that are vital to understanding this verse (and any text in the Bible).

- Always look at the context. Fundamental to understanding the text is ensuring that we read it in its context. In other words, we look at what comes before the text and after. We also need to be aware of the audience to whom the letter was addressed, the context in which it was written, and who was writing the letter.

One of the errors we can make in interpreting and understanding the Bible is to take a passage or a verse out of context. I have heard some people claim this verse in Philippians when they are facing some sort of challenge or crisis. They use it almost like a magical formula, repeating the verse over and over. But hold on a minute. Can we really do *all* things? No, I don't think we can. For example, saying the verse a million times won't change the fact that even though I would love to sing, I cannot. I wish I could scale heights, but I am not athletic, so no matter how often or how loudly I say this verse, it is not going to change the fact that I am not an athlete, and hence there are certain feats I will never accomplish.

Some people reading this devotion might not agree with my perspective on the text. Stick with me, and let me explain what this verse means in its context.

- Always read the preceding verses of the text. Let's read the preceding verses and then try to understand this particular one. As I mentioned, Paul was writing from prison, and he says in Philippians 4:12–13: "I know what it is to be in need, and I know what it is to have plenty. I have learned the secret of being content in any and every situation, whether well fed or hungry, whether living in plenty or in want. I can do all this through him who gives me strength." So then, what this verse means in its context is that we can find contentment whatever our circumstance is, whether we are full or hungry, whether things are going well or we are suffering; we can do all things because Christ strengthens us. Philippians 4:13 is not a scripture to encourage you to dream bigger dreams, but to take strength when those dreams are not fulfilled. Christ can give you the strength to endure when your dreams have failed and when part of God's plan includes suffering or hunger, as Paul experienced.

Being a Christian does not mean that we will not face challenges in life. In fact, Paul said in 2 Corinthians 11:24–27, "Five times I received from the Jews the forty lashes minus one. Three times I was beaten with rods, once I was pelted with stones, three times I was shipwrecked, I spent a night and a day in the open sea, I have been constantly on the move. I have been in danger from rivers, in danger from bandits, in danger from my fellow Jews, in danger from Gentiles; in danger in the city, in danger in the country, in danger at sea; and in danger from false believers. I have labored and toiled and have often gone without sleep; I have known hunger and thirst and have often gone without food; I have been cold and naked."

This sounds like a man who had broken dreams, adversity, persecution, and hardship beyond our ability to comprehend. And yet, through all his trials, he proclaims with triumph in Romans 8:35–39, "Who shall separate us from the love of Christ? Shall trouble or hardship or persecution or famine or nakedness or danger or sword? As it is written: 'For your sake we face death all day long; we are considered as sheep to be slaughtered.' No, in all these things we are more than conquerors through him who loved us. For I am convinced that neither death nor life, neither angels nor demons, neither the present nor the future, nor any powers, neither height nor depth, nor anything else in all creation, will be able to separate us from the love of God that is in Christ Jesus our Lord."

Some Christ followers have the misperception that they are entitled to every good thing and that whatever they claim in faith will be theirs. This is not the case, and I am unsure as to where they have read that particular concept in God's Word. From my reading of the Bible, Christians can and will go through struggles and trying times, but Jesus will strengthen them in the midst of those times.

Take courage today. If your dreams are shattered, and it feels as if life is coming undone, you are not alone. Paul knew exactly what trials felt like, and his exhortation is that we can find strength in Christ during these troublesome times. He will strengthen you for this part of your journey. Keep your eyes on Him.

Reflection

Write down what particular issue you need help with today. Ponder the reading in Romans 8, and commit to standing firm in your faith, no matter what the circumstances are. Write down Romans 8:38–39, and take the promise of God's eternal love with you into this day.

Prayer

God, I know that You hear my prayer. I come to You now and pray for the strength that I need for my day. I know that You can see me through my struggles and my pain, and I am asking You to help me to know Your strength and Your power in my life as I walk through this day. I know that there is nothing that can ever separate me from Your love.

Three Lessons Children Can Teach Us

 Reading: Matthew 18:1–9

I love children. Their innocence, trust, and vulnerability are all endearing characteristics. When Jesus wanted to teach His disciples about humility and His kingdom, He called a little child to show them what His kingdom looked like: "And he said: Truly I tell you, unless you change and become like little children, you will never enter the kingdom of heaven" (Matthew 18:3). There is something in a child that teaches us about the kingdom of God. When Jesus spoke about being like a child, He never implied that His disciples should be childish; rather, He was exhorting them to change and become childlike. To be childlike is different from being childish and immature. Simply put, it requires that simple trust I have been highlighting throughout this book. Let me try to expound this text by drawing out three principles that I think children can teach us:

- They have a capacity to trust. I love it when my grandchildren throw themselves into my arms, knowing that I will be there to catch them. They trust me. Jesus places a child in the midst of His followers to show them what trust looks like. I can see the picture in my mind. Jesus beckons the little child to come to Him. Shyly, the little one walks up to Him, looks lovingly into His eyes, knowing that she or he will be perfectly safe with Him. Simple childlike trust. To understand the kingdom of heaven is to grasp the simplicity of this type of faith. It is a certain knowledge that your God is there for you and that He loves you and will not fail you.

- They have a capacity to forgive. Sometimes, when my grandchildren have a squabble, their mom will rush into the room and say, "What is going on with the two of you?" It takes a bit of time to get to the bottom of the story, but eventually, she says to the guilty one, "Say sorry and then give each other a hug." The offender blurts out a hurried, "Sorry," to which the offended one then quickly replies, "I forgive you," and without any further ado, off they go and play as if nothing ever happened. I have always marvelled at a child's capacity to forgive and to forget. Jesus calls us to this kind of childlikeness because central to the life of the kingdom is forgiveness. Just as we have been forgiven by our heavenly Father, so, too, we need to forgive those who have offended us. This is not always easy, but for the sake of our soul's well-being, it is essential.

There is something important to understand about forgiveness. The act of forgiving does not always produce instantaneous results. Let me explain. Sometimes, when I forgive someone of a wrong committed against me, it requires a circuitous journey for me. I forgive them sincerely in my heart in that moment because I know that I must. However, a few days later, when I remember how they hurt me, anger or sadness wells up inside of me. I feel bad because I think I have not really forgiven them.

But that is not the case, because I did actually sincerely pray and ask God to help me to forgive the person who offended me. I have to stop and remind myself that I am human, and it is natural to feel hurt and at times even anger. However, I cannot stay in that frame because I need to walk daily in forgiveness. When anger fills my heart and Satan tries to condemn me and make me feel guilty at the failure in my Christian walk, I remind myself that I have forgiven that person, but I need to keep practicing forgiveness and walking in it on a daily basis. Sometimes, the process of forgiveness takes longer than the actual act of forgiveness. Be patient with yourself in the process.

- They have a capacity for adventure. A three-year-old child does not wake up and say to her mother; "Mom, leave me in bed. I am lying here, contemplating the effects of global warming." No, she jumps out of bed, ready for the first adventure of the day. Children have a wonderful capacity for adventure. As Christians, we should also have that kind of desire for new experiences. Live with expectancy, wondering what serendipity is around the corner. Get up in the morning and ask God, "What exciting things do You have in store for me today?" Have the sense of excitement that has you jumping out of bed and saying, "Whoopee! What adventures await me today?"

  I have an inkling that the kingdom of heaven is like that; it is an adventure. If you are bored, I would say that something is wrong. Jesus never intended for our lives to be monotonous. He wanted them to be full of joy and adventure, and I encourage you to develop an appetite for the exciting things God has in store for this day.

Children can teach us so much about the kingdom of heaven. The first thing they teach us is about simple trust. I want to learn from them. I hope you do. I pray that your capacity to trust and forgive will grow until forgiveness becomes as natural to you as breathing air. Above all, my prayer is that your life would be one incredible adventure. Enjoy today.

Reflection

Pause and think about your life for a few moments. Do you have that capacity for simple trust? What about forgiveness? Is there someone you need to forgive? Finally, is your life filled with adventure? I mean simple, daily, exciting serendipities? There is a lot to reflect on here, but write down, in as many sentences as you need, what you want God to do in your heart today.

Prayer

God, thank You for this new day. Thank You for challenging my heart. I open up my life to You and ask You to work graciously inside of me. I want to know You more. I want my life to reflect You, and I want to live a life that is filled with purpose. Please hear the prayer of my heart.

Character Counts

 Readings: Isaiah 32:1–8; 1 Corinthians 15:1–33

We are living in a strange world. Much has changed since I was a young person, and the world I grew up in is different from the one my grandchildren are living in. At times, people think and act in ways I am unaccustomed to. In one sense, it is true that everything is relative. Most people see the world through their eyes, which have been coloured by culture, personal experience, and their own worldview. However, Christ followers have proven through the centuries that certain values and norms can remain constant. At the heart of this is an understanding of the beauty, richness, and truth of God's Word as found in the Bible.

I recently read an article that suggested that good character can hinder a person and get in the way of them reaching the top. I have also heard arguments that suggest that upright character is not important, and that skills are what count in navigating life in the twenty-first century. It is clear that the moral landscape is changing in our world. As Christians, we face challenging times. Whilst a democratized society may legislate however it pleases, the belief in the church and its function creates a challenge for Christian people who seek to retain their moral compass in a society that seems to have none. It was Martin Luther King Jr. who prayed that his four little children would be judged by the content of their character and not by the colour of their skin. I couldn't agree more.

Then why do some people argue that character is not all that important? I would suggest that good character should still be our highest priority. And here is why I would argue that character still counts in the twenty-first century:

- Who you are is more important than what you do. We are human *be*ings, not human *do*ings. Simply put, what is inside of us or who we are is intrinsically more valuable than the tasks we accomplish. Yes, it is important to harness our skills and to work hard at doing the best in every situation. However, the importance of deep abiding character must never take second place.

  A Christian person with character and virtue should respond to issues such as classism, racism, sexism, or any other injustice in an appropriate way because their character has been shaped by the biblical narrative. They can make wise decisions because they are informed by the Bible, a story in which the essential components of love and justice are rooted and because they have learned and practised these virtues in the church. In turn, I hope that as Christians who believe that character is essential to who we are, we will influence society not through the imposition of a legal code but through lifestyles that reveal authentic Christian living.

- What you do is a result of who you are. The way I respond to every situation in life is determined by my character. Everything I do is based on who I am on the inside. I cannot act differently from the person I am internally. Perhaps there are times I can be a hypocrite and pretend, but in real-life situations, I am going to do what I am.

For example, kind people will commit kind acts. If you have lived in a family that values kindness and fairness, and if your elders modelled that value and you saw the fruits of kindness, then it will be a value you uphold in life. In other words, if you encountered a situation where someone was being bullied, your response would not be to bully them as well, but you would intervene in the situation with an act of kindness. As Christians, we should not seek to impose our morality on others in the hope of changing them, but rather seek to live an authentic life, believing that our actions will speak louder than our words.

- Good character matters. So from the example I just shared, most people would choose to live in a world where we valued kindness, justice, equity, and all those values that make human beings decent people. Sometimes, being a person of good character can have a cost associated it. Being honest can be costly in different scenarios. Standing up for right in a world with mixed values can cost us. Some people may never reach the top of their profession because honouring their values is more important than climbing a corporate ladder to earn more money. As I noted, Christians should not seek to impose their values on secular people. People who are not part of our Christian tradition will almost certainly not adopt our values or our morality. But when we live our lives in an authentic way that is a witness to society, I believe people are challenged by the sincerity of our lives. In other words, people will be more convinced by authentic lifestyles than by persuasive arguments. The world is without a doubt a better place because of authentic Christ followers.

The Bible places great import on the state of a person's heart. When all is said and done, I would rather work with a person of character than a person with skill. A person can have all the abilities in the world, but if they are unkind, unjust, untruthful, or unloving, then give me the person with character any day. Having said all that, when you marry skill with character, you have a powerful mix. Psalm 78:72 says it this way: "And David shepherded them with integrity of heart; with skillful hands he led them."

All around the world, there are hospitals, clinics, orphanages, and other community developments that have been set up by Christian people. And the world is a better place because of these institutions. Lives have been saved, abandoned children given homes, the sick given care, the elderly given respite because Christian people with godly values have sought to impact this world with God's kindness and love. Don't discount the influence that you can have on your world as a Christian. Find what God wants you to do, do it with all your heart, and live an authentic Christian life. See what God does to change your world.

Reflection

Write down ways in which you can model character in the place you live and work. What are two characteristics or virtues you would like to model in your life? In what ways do you think you could change your world in the coming months?

Prayer

God, help me to live in a way that honors You. I want to be a virtuous person who reflects You in everything I do and say. Help my life to shine before others so that when they see me, they see Jesus.

Punctuate Life

 Readings: Numbers 14; Joshua 14

Life is seldom boring; in fact, there are days I wish I could have a little bit of boredom. Weeks seems to run into each other, and before I know where I am, another year has vanished.

There are so many layers to our lives; at times, they are radiant with color, and almost in seconds, they can turn gray or even dark. One moment, we can be dancing with joy, and the next, we are facing challenges, struggles, or pain that we never anticipated. That is life. We never know what is around the corner; will it be a serendipity or a challenge? The point is, we have no idea what the day will hold.

Our lives are filled with different experiences, but we decide how to punctuate them. Do we put a period at the end of our experience or a question mark or a comma or even an exclamation? We are the ones who make the choice. As I mentioned in a previous devotion, Viktor Frankl, the German existentialist, said that in every situation of life, we make a choice. Although we cannot control the circumstances of our lives, we have absolute control over our responses to those circumstances.

A piece of writing without punctuation makes no sense. Life without punctuation does not have a whole lot of meaning, either. How we punctuate our lives is dependent upon us because we are the only ones who can determine where and how we choose to punctuate them. Just as punctuation gives clarity and meaning to our words, so too does the way you punctuate your life give meaning and purpose.

The Bible readings today give us some insight into the Israelite community and particularly into the lives of Joshua and Caleb. Joshua and Caleb had done everything they were asked to do by Moses. In an earlier devotion, you read Numbers 13 and 14. I encourage you to read these two chapters together so that you understand the context. These were two men who knew how to punctuate their lives correctly. And they did. When they came back from exploring the land that God had promised to them, they could have put a period at the end of that experience. The rest of the leaders had given a bad report and told Moses that exploring the land was one thing; inhabiting and claiming it was a different and impossible feat. Joshua and Caleb chose to punctuate their lives differently from the rest of the community. They punctuated life with a comma, believing there was more to come and another season to enjoy. The other ten chose to put a period at the end of this event. As a result, they never experienced the full plan of God or the joy of seeing His promise fulfilled. By contrast, Caleb and Joshua were the only two out of the twelve spies who inherited the land, even though it was some forty years later.

Let me explain some punctuation marks that people choose for their lives:

- Living with a question mark. I have seen people live with questions that sometimes have no answers. Why did this happen? Why me? What did I do wrong? Why did God allow this catastrophe? These are just some of the questions we ask that may never have answers, this side of eternity. There are mysteries that we do not understand, but a day will come when all will be revealed, and then everything will make sense. At the end of experiences that have probing questions, we need to decide what we are going to do to move forward with our lives. There are some questions that will never have the answers we want. We must decide if these unknowns will cripple us, or will we find God's peace despite the uncertainty? This is why the Bible speaks about the peace of God that passes all understanding. Eventually, we have to find peace, even if we don't have all the answers. This is a special grace that God gives to His people. Decide now that you will move on from the questions, and live in peace, knowing that God is good, and He knows the end from the beginning. The situation you are looking at may seem desperate, but remember: God is not finished yet.

- Living with a period at the end of pain. Some people live with a period at the end of a challenge, and they never move on from their pain. "Well," they say, "I am never going to let that happen to me again." They determine to lock out people and other experiences by putting a period after their struggle and pain. The only time there should be a period in your life is when it is over. Don't allow your pain to shape your tomorrow. Don't stop living an abundant life because of a bad or hurtful experience. Put the correct punctuation at the end of your hurt and move on. It may appear as if there will never be a new or exciting adventure again, but you need to set your sails for the wind.

I heard a story of an eighteenth-century missionary who set off to his new destination on a sailboat. One day, the captain knocked on his cabin door and said, "Sir, I know you are a man of prayer, and I have come to seek your help. There has been no wind now for many days, and from our readings, it appears that our ship is headed towards an island inhabited with cannibals. Please, would you pray that God would send wind so that we can set our course?"

The missionary said that he would certainly pray, but he had one request before he began interceding. "Captain," he said, "you must set your sails for the wind."

The captain was aghast and hastily responded, "Sir, there is not even a breath of air out there; my men would laugh at me for doing something that foolish." The missionary replied, "Well, then I cannot pray for wind."

The captain got the message and went out to set the sails for the wind. After some time, there was another knock on the cabin door.

The missionary opened the door to the captain who quipped, "Sir, could you please stop praying? We have more wind than we can handle."

Perhaps today is the day you choose to set your sails for the wind. I suggest you make a decision to replace the period you have placed in your life with a comma, look up, and know that God has a good plan for the rest of your life.

- Living with a comma. Life can be enriching and fulfilling, even if at times it is painful. Keep punctuating your life with a comma. When questions come that don't have answers, don't stop there; move on. When hurtful and challenging experiences fill your world, don't give up. There is more to life than we can imagine. Move past your pain and hurt, and determine that you are going to keep punctuating your life with color.

Joshua and Caleb could have punctuated their lives with question marks or even a period. Instead, they chose to believe God had a destiny for them. Yes, they waited for many years, but eventually, that destiny was fulfilled.

Never allow the unanswerable questions to hold you in their grasp. Allow each experience of life to teach you and then move forward. Take a deep breath, gain strength from the Lord, and then courageously move into this day and all that it holds for you.

(☼) Reflection

Spend some moments in quiet reflection. Has your life seemed to come to a halt because the pain and questions have been more than you could cope with? Be honest with yourself, and write down what experience has been punctuated with question marks or periods. Now ask God to help you to punctuate this period of your life with a comma so you can move on from it into the purpose and plan He has for you. You are never too old for new and exciting challenges. Perhaps your physical body is frail, but just as God used Caleb in his old age, He can use you. You may be young and feel as if life has already dealt you too many blows; please do not allow these experiences to stop you and hinder your tomorrow. Choose carefully how you will live this day and how you punctuate your life.

🙏 Prayer

God, help me to make wise choices today. I want to punctuate my life so that it resonates with the joy of Your plan and purpose. Help me to move beyond the questions and find peace in knowing that You are sovereign.

The Virtue of Small

 Reading: Judges 7

Big is beautiful, so we are told. If a town or church or organization is small, it is probably of little consequence or significance, so we are told. In the twenty-first century, it seems that you have to be big if you want to be reckoned with. Big is bold, significant, effective, influential, and powerful, or so we are led to believe. Some of the most influential and amazing people I know are unknown and unappreciated. It does not make them inconsequential because they are in the shadows. Gideon thought there was strength in numbers, until God showed him that numbers were not as important as having the Lord with him. This reading today is the story of how God helped Gideon conquer a large army with a small, bold, powerful group of obedient men.

Now before you think I am knocking big organizations or influential churches or high-powered individuals, hear me out, please. I am a great admirer of leaders who can gather thousands of people to their communities each week. It takes immense skill, gifting, and leadership to grow any community to thousands of people. I do think big churches and organizations can wield influence and power, and they can bless their cities and beyond because of their size and scope. I am keen to learn all that I can from these gifted people. This devotion is merely to show that there is as much virtue in small as there is in large. If you feel insignificant and unimportant, and if your life seems to be lived in the shadow of larger-than-life people, then this devotion is for you as well as anyone leading a small community or business.

- Small is not insignificant. If something is small or a person is in the shadows, that does not mean they are insignificant or lack the ability to influence. Just as big has many benefits and virtues, so too does small have virtues that we sometimes fail to appreciate.

  I live in a small state, in a tiny town, and by American standards, Paul and I lead a relatively small College. It took me moving to this tiny community to appreciate the impact that small can have. I love big; in fact, I think I prefer big, but I have also come to appreciate the virtue and influence of small. I marvel at the influence of many of the alumni who have gone from a small town to make a big impact in their world.

- Small should never cause feelings of inferiority. I have met pastors who lead small churches who feel inferior or intimidated by those who lead large and prosperous ones. I understand that some churches are small because their leaders are not diligent (or even worse are lazy). If a leader has a tiny congregation because they sit on their laurels, that is another issue altogether. That kind of small is insignificant, ineffective, and inconsequential. But if people lead a healthy, vibrant, small community, and they are putting their heart and soul into God's work, then I think they can be as influential in their communities as a large church and, sometimes, even more so. Likewise, a small family, a widow, or someone working in an obscure setting can have influence way beyond what can be imagined.

- Small should be celebrated. I seldom go to a conference or seminar where small is celebrated. As a rule, pastors of a big church or leaders of a large organization are asked to speak. I appreciate all the reasons why you would invite a person leading a large church to share their principles for growth. And I have been the beneficiary of many such conferences. However, the longer I live, the more I find I am learning from people who are working in smaller contexts. It would be helpful to be exposed to the stories of the incredible, gifted, significant, effective people leading small churches and organizations. Let us not silence the voice of the heroes who have heard God's call to what we consider insignificant places. Let us also applaud those humble enough to live, minister, and work in the shadows.

- Small is also in God's plan. Why did God choose a tiny, insignificant town like Nazareth for Jesus to be nurtured in? Why did He choose an insignificant girl from an unknown family to be the virgin who would carry the Messiah in her womb? Why didn't God send the great preacher, John the Baptist, to the big, bustling, vibrant city of Jerusalem? I ask myself, "Why would God send him to the desert?"

  Perhaps it is because God does and can use insignificant, isolated places and people of humble birth to make a great impact on His world. Do not despise small. I love big, but I also love small. God uses both.

If you are leading a small community, in an insignificant town, with few resources, hold your head high; you are God's chosen and anointed servant. You may never know the impact of your ministry, but if you are obedient and faithful, I can guarantee you that greatness surrounds you, and God is with you. If you are working in what appears to be an insignificant position, starting a small business or a member of a small church, pause and know that God sees you and has a plan for your life beyond what is currently visible.

⊛ Reflection

Whether you consider yourself or your ministry small or big, stop and pause to thank God for what you have. Now write down two goals you would like to achieve in this coming year. Spend some time reflecting on how you can achieve these goals.

🙏 Prayer

God, I know You are with me in my situation. I sometimes feel small and alone, but I know You are omnipotent and omnipresent, and in those two facts I take deep comfort. Help me to celebrate where I am and to yield every aspect of my life into Your hands. I do not seek significance for my own sake; I want to make You famous, and I pray You would use me to that end. Thank You for where You have placed me. I know that You see me, and in Your eyes, I am significant.

46

Reflections on the Worst Day of My Life

 Reading: Psalm 139

I have already said that memories are powerful recollections that can draw out all sorts of emotions from us. The emotions can be joy-filled reflections, or they can result in sadness, despair, or anger. Whatever emotion the memory triggers reminds us how powerful the stories of our past are and how deeply they can impact us. I am grateful for every memory I have. Whether the memory is a good one or a sad one, I have learned much of life from each experience. On reflection, I can truthfully say, I have grown internally more through the dark nights than I have through the sunny days.

I have shared this story many times, but now these years later, I sit here and reflect again on a day that I will never forget. I must reflect on this day because it initiated a period in my life that may grow dim with the passing years, but it must never be forgotten.

So allow me to share a memory from many years ago:

The doorbell rang, and as I hurried to open the front door, I was caught off guard by the burly policeman standing there. I smiled at him, waiting to hear the reason for why he was at my doorstep on this beautiful, sunny North Carolina day, the first day of July.

Without beckoning him to speak, he asked politely, "Is Jason Alexander your son?"

I replied in the affirmative, thinking that perhaps Jay had got a speeding ticket and that he felt it his duty to let me know. Without a pause, he then asked if he drove a black Mustang. Again, I answered in the affirmative.

Then the words seemed to tumble off his stammering lips, and one by one, they hit me with the force of a tornado: "Your son has been involved in a tragic accident.... You need to get to the hospital immediately."

Suddenly, my heart felt too big for my chest; all about me was dark. I felt as if I were sinking, but the unseen hand of Jesus was there; even if I did not feel it then, I know now that God was with me. He knew about this day, even though I did not. The psalm in our devotion today is one that I have referred to a number of times in this book; it has been a great comfort to me in times of distress. Psalm 139:16 says, "Your eyes saw my unformed body; all the days ordained for me were written in your book before one of them came to be." Nothing ever takes God by surprise. As surely as I knew anything, I believed that He would walk with me through the darkest valley I had ever traversed.

Our son fought for his life, and the dedicated medical staff of Carolina's Medical Centre fought alongside him. There were agonizing hours where I felt the pain of watching life ebb away from Jay was too much to bear. But God walked that journey with us, and never once did He leave us. I didn't always feel His presence, but I instinctively knew that He was there.

Jay had sustained a ruptured aorta, spleen, and liver; a rib had penetrated his heart; and another rib had penetrated one of his lungs. His entire rib cage had been smashed by the impact of a sixty-thousand-pound truck, traveling at sixty-five miles an hour, ploughing into the side of his car. At the scene of the accident, he was a G3 on the Glasgow Coma Scale, which in medical terms means no breathing, no pulse, and no visible sign of life. And thus began the longest most horrific journey of our family's life. I have written the full story in my book *Wild Hope: A Memoir.*

God spared Jay's life, despite the prognosis. He spent twenty-eight long days in Trauma ICU. Today, he lives a full and happy life in California. But let me reflect on this day and share a few lessons I learned.

- Life is short; seize each moment, and live to the full. We don't know about tomorrow. Today is all we have, so we need to make the most of every opportunity that comes our way.
- Don't carry the burden of bitterness or unforgiveness. I was so glad that when we faced this challenge with Jay, I did not have to think about who my enemies were. I knew my own heart was free, and I could focus every ounce of energy on praying for my son.
- Keep short accounts with people. It is so important to keep short accounts with people. Don't allow a wedge to grow between you and another person. Deal with the issues immediately. Life is too short to have an enemy. Learn the value of the word *sorry*. It will save you heartache in the years ahead.
- Stop and smell the roses. If Jay's accident taught me anything, it was to take time to smell the roses. Jay is a typical millennial, and Paul and I are from the boomer generation. Our generation drinks coffee on the run. Jay's generation makes coffee an experience. I have learned the delight of sitting in a coffee shop with Jay for over an hour (something I initially thought impossible as a boomer) and enjoying the ambience and the sheer joy of just being with my son. Don't miss the moment.

- Love deeply and live well. The deeper you love, the more pain you feel when someone is taken from you. But I am so thankful for the depth of love I feel for my family, my friends, and my community.

- Tell people how much you love and appreciate them. Perhaps you are not overtly affectionate and given to expressing words of appreciation. Change. People need to hear from you that they are loved and appreciated. It is as important for them to hear those words as it is for you to give them.

- Spend quality time with your family. In this fast-paced century, people and families are scattered across the globe. My family live on four continents, so I don't see them often. When we do spend time together, we make the most of every moment. We live, we laugh, we eat, we share stories, we cry, and most of all, we love.

- Love God with all your heart. I do not know what I would have done without my God. He is the One Who sustained me and kept me in my darkest night. When I felt as if I was slipping into a murky, muddy hole, His hand would reach down and lift me from my sorrow and draw me to Himself.

- Live each day as if it is the last, but plan for the years ahead. Live life to the full. Seize every moment of every day. Suck the marrow out of life, and then plan to live many more fruitful years.

Reflection

What have you learned from the traumatic days of your life? Pause and write down how your life has been impacted from this event. How do you want to live today? Write down some of the changes you wish to make in your life so you can take time to smell the roses.

Prayer

God, thank You for another day. Each day is a gift from You, another opportunity to live and influence and be influenced. Help me to live my life in a thoughtful way. Help me to learn from the past so that my future will be bright.

Enjoying the Season
You Are In

 Reading: Ecclesiastes 3

I don't want to end my life with regrets. When I breathe my last breath, I want to exhale with satisfaction, knowing that I lived well. Some of you reading this devotion may be younger than me, and some might be older, but whatever season you are in, I urge you to engage it to the full.

Living in North Dakota has accustomed me to living through the different seasons, and I appreciate each one. When we lived in Australia, the seasons were simply hot or hotter. It seems at times that you can have two or three seasons in a couple of weeks in North Dakota. Some nights, I lie in bed, listening to the wind howling and throwing sheets of rain from the sky, while thunder rumbles through the trees and echoes in my bedroom. I am accustomed to tropical thunderstorms, and I love the sound of thunder rolling through the skies while the earth greedily gulps down each and every drop that falls. I lie awake in those moments and revel in the sounds tumbling from the sky, knowing that I am safe and warm in my home.

A number of months ago, when I thought spring was just around the corner, I awoke to large, fluffy, white flakes of snow falling on the ground, threatening to dampen all hopes of spring. The week before, there were blossoms on the trees, and the sun was blazing in all its glory. One week later, we dropped 50 degrees in temperature and were blighted by snow. So we had winter in May.

Life is like that sometimes. Our lives are rolling along, and the air is full of hope and promise; spring is everywhere. And then one morning, we wake up, and *boom,* everything has changed. We find ourselves in the midst of winter. The problem is that most of us do not feel prepared for the sudden change of season. As Ecclesiastes 3:1–2 reminds us, "There is a time for everything, and a season for every activity under the heavens: a time to be born and a time to die, a time to plant and a time to uproot." The thrust of the chapter is that you discern the season you are in and navigate it with wisdom and care.

Every season has its own unique beauty. Spring is made all the more delightful because of winter's dark, cold days. I would never truly appreciate the sunshine if I had not been through the darkness of the night. Every season has its purpose, and each one can be meaningful if we internalize them and allow them to do their work in us. So how do we navigate the passing seasons?

- We cannot live in the past. I have to admit that I am somewhat of a sentimentalist. I sometimes long for the bygone days. We read in Philippians 3:13, "Forgetting what is behind and straining toward what is ahead, I press on toward the goal to win the prize for which God has called me heavenward in Christ Jesus." Instead of sitting and longing for yesterday, we have this day in front of us. This is the season we are living in now. Sitting and reminding yourself of yesterday won't help you to enjoy today. Remembering the hurts and licking your wounds won't help, either. Whatever the season you find yourself in, fall, winter, spring, or summer, engage it with passion and resolve.

- We cannot live in the future. When I was a young girl, I just wanted to finish school and go to college. When I was in college, I aimed to complete my studies so that I could get married. I got married and longed to have children. Once my children were born, I wanted them to grow so I would see what kind of adults they would become. Now, I find myself wondering where time went and wish I had taken the time to pause and enjoy each precious moment I had with my babies. Please enjoy this moment, and don't wish it away. Time is fleeting, and life is short. Some of us live only for tomorrow, for a future that may never come. The Bible talks about living for today. Tomorrow may have all sorts of exciting adventures for you, but you need to enjoy this day.

- We can only be certain of today. Seasons come, and seasons go. Each one has its own joys and challenges. The key is to maximize the moment you are in. We are never amiss to sit and reflect on past seasons. There is wisdom in reflection, but not in longing and pining for days gone by. When I am in the winter season of life, I reflect on the glory of spring, reminding myself that winter may strip the trees naked, leaving them exposed to the elements, but spring is around the corner, and soon those trees will clothe themselves in glorious green leaves.

Growing old is a privilege that many people do not get, so don't despise your gray hair and wrinkles because they are evidence of a life lived, trials overcome, and victories won. You may not be as flexible or as mobile as you used to be, but you have collected experiences along the way, and you are endued with wisdom. You learned that relationships are far more important than things and discovered that money does not buy you happiness. As time goes by, you savor the moment, knowing that most circumstances are out of your control, so you learn to accept things that come your way. The peace and joy in this season are different and unique. As life wears on, you find yourself becoming more comfortable in your own skin because you have nothing to prove.

So if you are in this season of life, stop to thank God for the privilege of growing old. Grow old gracefully, and don't fight it, but accept it as part of the journey of life. However, for those who are in the springtime of life, be wise with your time. Do not constantly wish time away. Pause, breathe deeply, exhale slowly, and thank God for this season right now.

(✍) Reflection

Pause to think about the season you are in. Write down the benefits of this particular season you are living through. What can you do to enhance this time of your life? Think of three things you are grateful for about this season, and then stop to pray.

🙏 Prayer

God, I am thankful for the season I am in right now. Thank You for bringing me to this point in my life. I ask for wisdom to use my time wisely. I pray for grace to live in the present, not in the past or the future. Help me through this season as I transition to the next.

Your Beautiful Mind

 Readings: Romans 12; Philippians 4:6–7

The human brain is an amazing organ with over 100 billion neurons; it is a complex and intricate creation. Scientists tell us that we have not even begun to tap the full capacity of the brain. They say that the brain loses an average of 85,000 neurons a day, but be encouraged; there are 40 billion other neurons available in your cerebral cortex for you to make use of.

My sister had a stroke a number of years ago that impacted her body in different ways. There were parts of her right side that were paralyzed, but through sheer determination and hard work, she has regained full use of those affected areas. Over time, the neural pathways repaired themselves, and she now leads a normal life, much as she did before her stroke. The brain is an amazing organ.

Your brain is a living organ that grows and expands as you learn, walk, communicate, and pray. Don't ever underestimate the power of your brain. So why is the brain so important?

- Your brain has potential to improve. You may be getting older, but you can still learn new things. You are never too old to learn and to grow. If your brain has been damaged by a stroke or some unfortunate accident, you can find new neural pathways to restore functions that were impaired. Did you realize that meditation is good for the health of the brain? Praying is not only a way to communicate with God, but it also has a powerful and positive affect on your brain. Reading and meditating on scripture can also significantly help your brain. It always makes me smile that what some scientists do not realize is that their so-called discoveries are not new to God, and many of them are principles we glean from the Bible. The apostle Paul gave us advice in Romans 12:2: "Do not conform to the pattern of this world, but be transformed by the renewing of your mind. Then you will be able to test and approve what God's will is—his good, pleasing and perfect will." In other words, if you want to change your life, you need to have your mind transformed.

Scientific experiments have shown that physical exercise can improve the function of your brain. Just walking for twenty minutes a day will revitalize you and also replenish neurons in your brain. So if you enjoy walking and praying, you are definitely improving your brain.

- Your brain has the ability to delete experiences. That sounds a little far-fetched, but actually, you can unlearn certain things. On the surface, this may appear a strange concept, but scientists now say that our brain has a type of delete button. If we train our brains to stop thinking about a negative experience and begin to think about positive experiences, we can delete some of those memories that haunt us. It sounds complicated, but the process is actually simple. Colossians 3:2–3 says, "Set your minds on things above, not on earthly things. For you died, and your life is now hidden with Christ in God." It is a deliberate act on our parts to replace the old information in our brains with new and good information.

- Your brain has the ability to improve your physical well-being. It is true that what people think impacts the whole of their being. As a psychology student, I learned how negative thought processes in the brain impact physical well-being, and those thoughts upset the balance of hormones in the body, which can undermine the immune system. Chronic stress can not only diminish your life, it can also decrease its length. This is why it is important to keep our brains healthy. Scientists have also shown how random acts of kindness do marvels for the brain, as do strong and healthy relationships. These really are some simple solutions to keeping your brain healthy and your mind beautiful.

Our Creator Who fashioned us has given our brains these wonderful capacities to learn, to create, to reflect, and to grow. Two thousand years ago, an expert in the law asked Jesus a question: "'Teacher, which is the greatest commandment in the Law?' Jesus replied: 'Love the Lord your God with all your heart and with all your soul and with all your mind.' This is the first and greatest commandment. And the second is like it: 'Love your neighbour as yourself.' All the Law and the Prophets hang on these two commandments" (Matthew 22:36–40). Loving God with every part of our being, and loving our neighbors, not only assures us of life after death, but of a peace-filled life on earth. God knew that loving Him and other people is not only good for us but is essential to the well-being and health of our minds. Don't waste your mind; it is a beautiful gift from God. Keep your brain healthy by fostering strong relationships with people, by feeding your mind with wholesome thoughts, by being a lifelong learner, and by dwelling on all the good aspects your life. And above all this, love your God with every fiber of your being.

Reflection

Is your mind filled with anxiety, negativity, or worry? Pause and ask God to help you. Now write down some steps that you will take to improve the health of your mind.

Prayer

God, I thank You that I am fearfully and wonderfully made. You formed me, and You know me better than I know myself. I ask You for Your help today in enabling me to think thoughts that help my brain to grow and be the beautiful, complex organ you made it.

Who Will Capture the Minds of Our Children?

 Reading: Deuteronomy 6

In October 2015, *Playboy* (a monthly American men's magazine) announced that it would "cease the publication of nude photographs of women in its magazine." When I read this, I said, "Great news." But was it really good news? Morally, it appeared to be a positive report; however, when we delve into the details, we discover something different. The editor of *Playboy* had not had a change of heart; rather, the magazine's publishers declared that their product was no longer viable. The reason was telling: Pornography is so pervasive and freely accessible on the internet that people no longer bought their product.

The CEO of *Playboy*, Scott Flanders, had this to say: "You're just one click away from every sex act imaginable for free. And it's just passé at this juncture." Two years later, Cooper Hefner, the son of Hugh Hefner (founder of the magazine), reneged on that decision, and the magazine continued publishing as before.

There are a number of challenges that we face as a society. The issue of human trafficking is an ever-increasing problem, as many women are forced into sexual slavery. Women living in the twenty-first century are more afraid of rape in our society than previously, and the statistics reveal that many rapists have spent prolonged periods of time viewing pornography. That places a whole new perspective on the power of pornography. I understand that at a certain age, people can choose to view what they want. But does that make pornography right? Does that create a wholesome society? Does it strengthen marriages and help families? I think not.

Children and teenagers can access the internet via their phones, computers, and tablets whenever they choose. The saddest part of this story, for me, is that even *Playboy* has lost its shock value for teenagers. They are able to access anything and everything they want on the internet. The impact of these images has far more devastating consequences than we can imagine.

So what can we do to protect our children and young people? I will make a few suggestions:

- Pray for your young people. As trite as this sounds, I do believe we need to pray for our children and teenagers more than ever. They are vulnerable. Today's teenagers know more about sex than they should. The power and beauty of two people loving each other and committing themselves to one another for a lifetime is a foreign concept to many of this generation. Our children need to learn from their parents that marriage is a lifetime commitment between two people. I understand that relationships can go sour, and divorce is one of the sad consequences, but that should not stop parents from instilling in their children the importance of commitment to another person and the value of keeping our vows.
- Watch out for your children. Know where your children are and who their friends are. I am not saying we cut them off from their friends, but it's imperative that we know the

places that our children frequent and what activities they are involved in.

- Invest time in your children. We need to spend time with our children and warn them against some of the dangers of the internet. I have seen families spending time together, but every single member was on their phone or i-Pad. That is not quality time together. They might be in the same room physically, but they are not really present. Family and devotion times are important disciplines that can help you and your children to navigate the cultural challenges they face. Raising children to become healthy adults is a 24/7 task. This is not merely a Sunday event. Our reading exhorts us to impress these teachings on our children; when you go for walks, talk to them about God, show them His beautiful creation, remind them that He made everything. Teach them to appreciate beauty by appreciating all the Lord's handiwork. Talk to them about respecting others, and show them how that is done. When you put them to bed at night, remind them of God's goodness, and when they rise in the morning, remind them of His faithfulness.

- Speak openly with your children. Let your children feel safe with you. They should be secure coming to you with their questions and concerns. They need to know that they can come and talk to you at any time, about anything. It is far safer that they get their information from loving, godly parents than from friends who have tainted values or from an unwholesome conversation on a school bus or an unsavory site on the internet.

- Don't rely on others to guide your children. Training a child in the things of God is first and foremost the role of a parent. Their teachers can be a help in assisting in the role, but it is primarily a parent's responsibility.

- Lead your children by example. Don't tell your children one thing and do another. This passage exhorts us as parents to love God and put Him first in our own lives. Some parents want godly kids, but they don't have personal discipline in place in their own lives. If you want your children to read God's Word and live accordingly, then lead the way. Let your faith be public; it is not a private affair. Deuteronomy 6:9 says, "Write them on the doorframes of your houses and on your gates." In other words, your faith should be lived out loud before everyone, not only your community of faith. Teach your children to live out their faith before their friends. They should never be shy about sharing Jesus with others.

- Ensure your children are filling their minds with good material. It is important to have a daily family devotion. Start and end your day with God. Help your kids to memorize texts from the Bible. When temptation comes, they have God's Word buried in their hearts, and it can help them to make the right choices. Psalm 119:9 says, "How can a young person stay on the path of purity? By living according to your word." The psalmist augments his statement by adding, "I have hidden your word in my heart that I might not sin against you" (Psalm 119:11). One great gift you can give your children is a love for the Bible.

Reflection

Pause and say a prayer for the children and young people in your family. Is there anything you can do to help them navigate some of the cultural challenges of their day? Write them down. Now commit to pray for them and to keep to the commitment you have written.

🙏 Prayer

God, I bring my children and teenagers before Your throne today. I know You love them as much as, if not more than, I do. I ask You to give me wisdom in guiding them along the straight path. I pray for a bright future for each one of them. Please help them to navigate the challenging days in which they live. I ask You to nudge my heart when I need to pray for them. Keep them safe and close to You, I pray.

Homeward Bound

 Readings: Psalm 84; Revelation 21

You would think by the way some people gather possessions and property that they were going to live forever. The truth is that life is short. And while I am a great believer in living life to the full, I know that I am living for a future far grander and more wonderful than I can comprehend. I am ultimately bound for eternity.

The psalm in our reading today is one of my favorites. The psalmist begins by proclaiming, "How lovely is your dwelling place, Lord Almighty! My soul yearns, even faints, for the courts of the Lord; my heart and my flesh cry out for the living God" (Psalm 84:1–2). What a majestic and positive declaration to start the day. He says his soul, his entire being, longs for the Lord Almighty. Further on, the psalmist continues, "Blessed are those whose strength is in you, whose hearts are set on pilgrimage" (Psalm 84:5). I love the picture the psalmist paints for us in this text. It is the picture of pilgrims whose hearts long after their God. It is a beautiful tapestry of a life that is totally committed to the Lord. The psalm ends in a crescendo: "Lord Almighty, blessed is the one who trusts in you" (Psalm 84:12).

I can think of no better way to finish this devotional book than to point you to the ultimate goal of every Christ follower. Undoubtedly, the psalmist had eternity in his sights. He knew that he was merely a pilgrim passing through. As such, he was trusting God with his life and knew that God would turn the Valley of Baka into a place of springs because the autumn rains would cover it with pools. As pilgrims, we will go through valleys, but God can turn them into places filled with springs.

Sometimes, our lives can feel dismal, like cold air creeping under the blanket and clinging to your naked skin. The sky looks bleak like dishwater, but winter finally gets weary of herself, and when the gentle snow, like flour through a sieve, finally stops falling, it gives way to a fresh breeze, pouring into your soul, bringing delicious coolness and relief as to a stuffy room.

So we are homeward bound. What does that mean? How should we live?

- Set your hearts on pilgrimage. I have no idea what heaven is going to be like. I can imagine, but I am certain that even in my wildest imaginings, it will not compare with what God has prepared for me. The book of Revelation gives us brief glimpses into what heaven will be like. "He will wipe every tear from their eyes. There will be no more death or mourning or crying or pain, for the old order of things has passed away" (Revelation 21:4). Some of you have family and friends who have already moved to their heavenly home. They are safe, secure, happy, pain free; they are home. If your eye is on the next purchase or the next achievement, let me encourage you to lift your sights higher. You are simply a pilgrim passing through this life. We are actually eternal beings bound by time and space, but one day, we will break through these earth-bound barriers, and then our pilgrimage will be over. We will be home.

- Focus on the goal. The ultimate goal is heaven. I understand that we must live our lives and engage them fully, but we also need to keep the main thing, the main thing. John 14:1–3 says, "Do not let your hearts be troubled. You believe in God; believe also in me. My Father's house has many rooms; if that were not so, would I have told you that I am going there to prepare a place for you? And if I go and prepare a place for you, I will come back and take you to be with me that you also may be where I am." What a comforting truth this is. In essence, what Jesus is encouraging us to do is to keep our eye on the ultimate goal and, in so doing, keep our focus on Him. The writer to the Hebrews said it this way: "And let us run with perseverance the race marked out for us, fixing our eyes on Jesus, the pioneer and perfecter of our faith" (Hebrews 12:1). My friend, God has already mapped your race out from start to finish. Don't get distracted along the way; keep your eyes on Jesus.
- Finish well. How will your story end? I know I ask myself that question on a regular basis. I don't want to hobble up to the finishing line. I want to go running through, straight into my eternal abode. As I breathe my final breath here on earth, I know Jesus will be waiting for me and will take my hand and welcome me home. My dear friend, live well, keep your eye on the goal, but more importantly than all of that, finish your race well.

My ardent prayer is that you the reader will be challenged and encouraged to live well. I trust that a daily devotion will become part of the rhythm of your life. Above all, I pray that you will keep your eyes on this magnificent Jesus I have spoken about. He gave His life for you, my friend, and He wants your life on earth to be rich and full, and finally, His desire is to welcome you into eternity when you have accomplished all He has for you on this earth. Be blessed.

⊛ Reflection

Ponder John 14:2 again. If you were to die today, would you be ready to meet your Maker? This is the most important question I can ask you. Be honest with yourself. Has your life gone around in endless circles? Perhaps you are reading this because Jesus is trying to capture your attention. If you have never opened your heart and life to Jesus, please pray the prayer below.

🙏 Prayer

God, thank You for sending Jesus to this earth. I know and understand that He died for my sins so that I could have a full life. Jesus, I invite You into my life right now. I ask You to cleanse me from my failures, flaws, and faults. You know them better than I do. I know that You made me and that You love me, and now, I want to love You and follow You in return. I am opening my heart and my life to You right now. I welcome You to become the Lord of my life. I am tired of doing things my way, I want to live my life for You. Help me to keep my commitment to follow You all of my days. And now, I thank You for hearing and answering this simple prayer. Amen.

Author's Note

My life has been an incredible adventure, and I attribute the success and joy of my journey to Jesus. When I met Paul, I was immediately attracted to him because I knew that He loved the Lord as much as I did. One thing we have always understood in our marriage is that Jesus would come first. And He has. We have committed our entire lives to serving this amazing God that we both met as young people. Because we made the decision to put God first in our lives, we have been blessed with a wonderful and happy marriage for over four decades.

Our lives have been fraught with challenges, and some of those I have shared quite honestly with you. I have also spoken openly about some of my raw moments of pain. St. Augustine said, "In my deepest wound I saw your glory and it dazzled me." I have been dazzled by God's glory for over four decades now, and it is true to say that my trials have made me more aware of His beauty than anything else.

I have written this book hoping that divulging some of the challenges of my life would encourage you, the reader, in your journey. I have no greater desire than that all people, everywhere, would come to experience this amazing God Who has colored my life with so many beautiful shades.

Our family are all followers of Jesus, and it gives me great joy to know that their lives are being lived for Him. Although we all live at a great distance from each other, we spend as much time together as possible. Every Christmas, we all get together in North Carolina to celebrate the season. We share wonderful, happy moments and end our time for one week together at the beach. All of us enjoy walking, swimming, playing tennis, cooking together, eating, and playing endless games of Monopoly, Scrabble, Clue, and UNO.

I trust that this devotional has not only blessed your life but has also been helpful to you. Some of the devotions have been raw and honest, and I hope that the challenges in the book will produce good fruit inside you, the reader. These devotions have been written over months, but the experiences I shared have been part of a six-decade journey.

Sometimes, I read a book and get frustrated because I wonder how so many amazing miracles could occur in one book. I have to remind myself that I can read a book in a couple of weeks, but the stories they tell take a lifetime of living. There are only fifty devotionals in this book, but each experience shared has been months and years in the process of being lived. Be patient with yourself as you work through some of the challenges in your life. Remember that God is with you.

I am grateful for so many things: my amazing children and grandchildren, the love of my life, Paul, and above all of that, my amazing God. I do believe that we can love other people more when we love God the most. Following Jesus is not about a commitment to some moral code; it is about loving Him, enjoying Him, and living the life He has destined for you.

I am and always will be,
Recklessly abandoned, ruthlessly committed, and in relentless pursuit of Jesus.
Carol

Carol with her grandchildren

Printed in the United States
By Bookmasters